THE
GOLDEN AGE
OF WISCONSIN

AUTO
RACING

Photos and text
by Father Dale Grubba

Badger Books Inc.
Oregon, Wisconsin

Published by Badger Books Inc.
Printed by McNaughton & Gunn of Saline, Mich.

Some material previously published by the Rev. Dale Grubba under the titles of *Dream Chasers* and *Wisconsin's Finest.*
Articles authored by Rev. Dale Grubba and reprinted by permission of *Stock Car Racing Magazine* include: "Dick Trickle: The Man," August 1988; "He's Got the Special Touch" (Al Schill), December 1988; "Joe Shear: The Great Midwest Star Has Passed On," June 1998; and "Who Is This Guy Matt Kenseth?" July 1998.
The publisher thanks Tim Saterfield for his technical assistance.

ISBN 1-878569-67-8

Badger Books Inc.
P.O. Box 192
Oregon, WI 53575
Toll-free phone: (800) 928-2372
Web site: http://www.badgerbooks.com
E-Mail: books@badgerbooks.com

Contents

Introduction

"You have got to come over to the Wisconsin Dells Speedway and see what is going on. It is unbelievable!" It was that invitation that got this seminarian, home on summer vacation, involved in racing in the early sixties.

What was happening at the Speedway on Saturday nights was truly incredible. I have always felt that if you were born to love racing you could not have asked for a better place to be born than central Wisconsin in the sixties and seventies.

Marlin Walbeck, who had begun his career in the 1950's, was trying to hold his position against a young generation — Dick Trickle, Tom Reffner, Jimmy Back, Marv Marzofka, Evert Fox, Rich Somers, Dave Fields, and a host of others.

The cars varied in make and model. There were coupes, sedans and even a station wagon. The components were stock, most salvaged from the local junkyard. It didn't take long to become hooked.

It was a hot summer day, perhaps that same vacation, and I was standing in a farm yard next to Highway 51 the main artery from northern to southern Wisconsin. The speed limit at the time was 65. I watched as this black stub nosed '56 Chevrolet hauler crested the hill with its tire rack sticking over the cab. The short bed held that black and gold racer. A racer with no front fenders, the hood under the tire rack. The hauler seemed to fly by on its way to the races in Oregon, Wisconsin, to do battle with Don and Rudy Eandt, Ed Fume, and Johnny Ziegler.

I watched in awe as Walbeck stood exhausted in

winner's circle after winning the biggest show of the time, the Rockford National Short Track Championship in the fall of 1967. I watched him build his '65 Chevelle and his final '69 Chevelle in Herman Smith's welding shop in Rib Lake. Innovations of the day were airplane gas and left rear tires filled with water.

My friend of that era idolized Richard Petty and dreamed of being a race driver. He bought a red Plymouth Barracuda with a loud exhaust, black racing stripe from front to back. Together we made plans to build a Dodge with a hemi engine. We pulled the car to the farm from a neighboring salvage yard and gutted it out. A neighboring farmer welded a black pipe roll cage in it.

Finishing touches, like the #14 had been painted on the side of it, when he appeared at my dad's farm to announce that he would not be driving it. He mysteriously left Wisconsin and wouldn't return for a number of years.

In the meantime I took my parents to every race at the Dells. We sat in the same spot every week and knew everyone that surrounded us. Soon we were making occasional visits to Adams-Friendship, Tomah-Sparta and Wisconsin Rapids. The drivers and owners who frequented those tracks raced under the banner of the Central Wisconsin Racing Association. The CWRA had one interest — good racing. Every night I wrote down the top three in the feature and semi-feature and at the end of the season typed it up on a clean sheet of paper. It was posted on the bulletin board over my desk each winter provoking dreams of the summer to come.

One of the saddest nights of my early lifetime occurred on a Labor Day Weekend just before my return to the seminary. It was pouring rain at the farm but I loaded my parents in my '53 Chevrolet for the 14 mile trip to the Dells. It couldn't be raining there. When we arrived the parking lot was empty. There wasn't a soul present. We pulled up to the gate and through steamed windows read, "Closed for the season."

The CWRA circuit became my home for much of the sixties and seventies. Wednesday night was LaCrosse, Thursday night Wausau, Friday night Madison or Adams-Friendship, Saturday night Wisconsin Dells and Sunday night Griffith Park. Tuesday nights became a night for specials.

For Dick Trickle and CWRA regulars the total number of programs run in a year easily reached 100. Those feats were accomplished with one car and one engine.

"I remember one Saturday night they hauled half my car off the track with one wrecker and the other half off with another wrecker. Sunday afternoon I raced again," says Trickle.

After I was ordained in 1966, I was teaching and summers were relatively free. The promoters at the Dells asked me to do invocations and the idea spread until whatever track I showed up at I was invited to do so. It didn't take long and I had my own racing column in the *Checkered Flag Racing News.*

Every night the same talented drivers squared off. It was an era of A and B features. "Everybody wanted to be a hot dog," Marv Marzofka recalls.

Features were 25 laps, 50 and 100 on holidays and at specials. Fields were inverted and the racing was phenomenal. But it wasn't just the racing. There was a spirit of camaraderie among the drivers.

"They talk about the roaring twenties," says Trickle. "Someday they may compare the twenties to our era and find the twenties coming up short."

Half the fun of going to the races in those days was sitting around listening to the stories about what was happening away from the track.

In one of those sessions at the close of the season at Golden Sands, Lyle Nabbefeldt gave me a beer. I told him I would save it and, during the winter at the conclusion of a day that had been particularly exasperating, I would dig it out of the back of the refrigerator and drink it and think of the good times we had the summer before. I did.

Grubba

It was the first race of the year at Golden Sands and I was leaving the pits thinking of the two-hour drive and getting home at 3 a.m. Up on the hill I could see Lyle and the other drivers. If I went up to tell him that I had drank the beer and how much it had meant to me it would be even later by the time I got home. I wavered and then I did it.

It was the last time I ever spoke to Lyle. Lyle would die in a crash in turn one at the Dells on a Memorial Day weekend.

That era of racing is gone but I am glad to have been a part of it. This book covers many of those years when the CWRA was growing and at its peak. The CWRA, so powerful in that era, no longer runs on a regular basis at any track. ARTGO, now the RE/MAX series, ASA, NASCAR Truck, Busch Grand National give talented drivers, like Matt Kenseth, the opportunity to move up quickly.

Except for a few, like Scott and Chris Wimmer, whose dad remembers the days of old, few drivers run more than two or three nights a week. Many choose to run specials. The power base is no longer Wisconsin Rapids but Madison, Kaukauna and Slinger. Racing is still great in Wisconsin but time moved on.

And my grade school friend. He returned one day from an uncharted journey across the United States induced by mental illness. He was driving an old Dodge, the remnant of a dream. Claiming he was Christ landed him in a mental institution, the subject of shock treatments. Released for a day to attend his uncle's funeral, he took his own life.

The Dodge race car, with its hemi engine, sits in the trees behind the machine shed at the farm. Whenever I look at it, I think of how much he loved the sport he introduced me to and, thinking of my own life and involvement in racing, how much he has missed. He might have been another Richard Petty.

— **Father Dale Grubba**
June 2000

The first gypsies

From the beginning of time we have been able to run with the best of them. It is like Keokuk, Iowa, with Ernie Derr, Ramo Stott and Don White," Jere O'Day said as he pulled his right leg up on the back bar at his pub and reflected on three generations of Wisconsin Rapids area racers and the legacy they helped fashion.

Gray-bearded Don Ruder agreed: "In those days, we had some skilled drivers. Rapids' drivers made a good showing wherever they went, and it is still the same. The racing people around here are good, fierce competitors."

For men like O'Day, the Second World War had just ended, but it didn't take long for another cause to surface, a passion that would last several decades. It was an era of dirt tracks, hundred dollar cars, and a case of beer for a rollover. "I wasn't trying to prove anything. The pay wasn't great. I just loved doing it." Then O'Day tries to explain what can't be explained: "It is like a sickness. I once saw a pregnant wife with a little boy in tow walk up to her husband and give him an ultimatum. The guy had just smashed his car twice, and he wasn't going to make it no matter what, but he still told her he would give her up before the car." Barnstorming. You have to be a good gypsy to do it. Race. Drive all night. Race the next day.

Many of the area drivers got their start at Crown's Speedway, a high-banked quarter-mile just out of Wisconsin Rapids on Highway 54. It was there that Red

Nichols, Jerry Bredl, Don Ruder, Augie Winkleman, and 50 or 60 more tested each others' skills on a regular basis.

Of all those drivers, Augie Winkleman stands out. "Augie didn't know what he was going to do from one lap to the next, so how was anyone else supposed to know?" asked O'Day. "At Wausau he pushed his own son over the back bank. If he would do that to his own son, you can imagine what his thoughts were about the rest of us. He wiped me out once, and I waited three years to get even. I looked in the rearview mirror and here comes Augie. I just decided, 'Augie, today is your day.'"

Even Dick Trickle, who raced against Augie in the twilight of his career, has vivid memories. "He was crazy, just furious. He drove like he was in a rage, banging and bumping everyone. It was as if every time he buckled his helmet, he was already going 100 mph plus."

It was to Crown's Speedway in 1950 that Jere O'Day towed his first car, a 1935 Ford coupe. "I donated the car and someone else was supposed to drive it. When we got to the track, the supposed driver chickened out and said, 'You drive it!' The first night out, my front end got knocked off and the second night I rolled it."

For six years, O'Day toured the local dirt circuit. "I loved those dirt tracks, like the Speedbowl in LaCrosse, where the sand was two-feet deep. No one could see. It was my kind of racing."

It had its bumps as well as good times: "I broke an axle at Wausau and went end for end. They took me to the hospital, but I pulled a disappearing act and was at Crown's Speedway to race that evening. My wife couldn't believe it. I had fast time, won the heat, and finished second in the feature!"

In 1956, he hooked up with mechanic Minnow Moll and for three years toured the IMCA circuit. Ralph Richardson and Don Lemis bought two Kiekhaefer Fords. They were the same type of car in which Norm Nelson and Tim Flock had won titles.

"I drove a 1956 Ford for Richardson and then bought the car," O'Day recalled. "We followed the fairs... Shreveport... Houston... north to LaCrosse and Minneapolis and then out west into the Dakotas. The only time we came home was for a fresh motor.

"The competition was Ernie Derr, Don White and Johnny Beauchamp, who came in second in the first Daytona 500. I remember Ramo Stott's first race. Talk about a gypsy outfit, but look where he ended up!"

Travel was extensive and payoffs low, but a love for racing seemed to pull the drivers from one track to the next. "Once, when the Ford broke, we drove all the way back to Waupaca to get a Kiekhaefer Dodge that was really a nothing car and drove all the way back to Hutchinson, Kansas to race. I couldn't even steer the car. Then Minnow discovered a broken key in the steering column mechanism, but I still didn't do anything.

"I was going to hang it up, but then I had a few drinks with Lenny Funk, and the next thing I knew I had made up my mind to go to Oklahoma City. We were traveling along late at night and all of a sudden a head gasket blows in the tow car. Minnow and I limped into the nearest motel and decided to get a night's sleep. We couldn't figure out why there were cars coming and going around that motel all night. Then, the next morning, we discovered that it served as a place of prostitution. We got the tow car fixed, got to Oklahoma City and I timed in sixth, which was way over my head.

"In the race, I passed everyone on the first lap and decided to ride the guardrail. It worked until I hooked it and started spinning. If there were 33 cars in the race, 33 hit me. I came to a halt with the right front wheel bent over. Minnow came running up to let the air out of the inner tube and save it. The tire blew and flipped Minnow over backwards. The next day we won $500. We ended up leaving the car in Davenport."

In 1959, O'Day returned to race a 1939 Ford locally. "Sam Bartus had just opened Griffith Park, and I won seven races in a row, rolled the car, and then won two

The author, Father Dale Grubba, became a fixture at central Wisconsin tracks and he often was asked to bless the cars.

more. I won every feature held there that year."

The end was near and a new hero would soon arrive from Rib Lake, Wisconsin. "Marlin Walbeck had been racing an old Dodge," O'Day recalled. "Then he and Mogie Dahl teamed up to build a Chevrolet. It put the finishing touches on the rest of us. The next year, Mogie built a Chevy for Jerry Bredl and I drove it, but it was the last year that I had a fast car."

MARLIN WALBECK

The pride
of Rib Lake

After Marlin Walbeck had seen his first race in the 1940's, there was no rest. He was going racing. The first car, a 1938 Ford, cost $50 and he paid for it by cutting and selling cedar posts. His first race was in Merrill against the top drivers of that time — Gus Winkleman of Merrill and Red Nichols of Wisconsin Rapids. Russ Sukow gave him a reason to remember that race.

"It was a 20-lap feature, and I spent more time off the track than on it, primarily because Gus kept hammering on me," Walbeck said. "Racing was unbelievably rough in those days! It took me years to get even with Sukow, but I did it one night at Minocqua. There was a hole in one section of the track, and I knew if he got up alongside of me I could come bouncing out of that hole and make it look like an accident. I did and tore his front wheel right off."

Interrupted by some years spent in the Army, Walbeck returned to racing in the early 1950's and began a career that would stretch into the late 1960's.

Like others, Walbeck chuckles at the mention of the name of one of his early dirt opponents, Augie Winkleman. "He had glasses that were thicker and contained more welding specks than Jimmy Back's! Augie would trip over jacks and equipment in the pits. In a race car he could drive right into the side of you and

13

claim, 'I never saw you!' In those days, we hauled our cars on trailers and on one particular night my tow car broke down. Along came Augie and hooked my trailer up to his car and trailer. It was all right when we were traveling 35 mph, but when we got up to 60, I didn't even want to look around. Way back there was my trailer, just snaking around looking as if it might break loose at any moment. Cars coming the other way were

Marlin Walbeck

going in the ditch, but it didn't bother Augie."

Some of Walbeck's other dirt opponents included Bill Bernhagen, Harold Mueller and Mogie Dahl, who would later build engines for Walbeck.

But it wasn't long before Marlin heard of the paved Griffith Park in Wisconsin Rapids. Switching to pavement proved to be to his liking, and it was here that he made his name, although he never lost his love for dirt racing. Even in his later years, he would kid Dick Trickle and Marv Marzofka about "loosening it up and running at the Marshfield fair."

Between that first 1938 Ford and the final 1969 Chevrolet, Walbeck sat in many home-built cars produced in Herman Smith's Rib Lake welding shop. Before his career ended, he had raced in a 1940 Ford, a 1938 Dodge, a 1955 Chevy, a 1956 Chevy, three 1957 Chevys, a 1965 Chevelle and, the last, a 1969 Chevelle. The best were the 1957 Chevys and his best years were 1964-1966. One of those 1957 Chevys, built for $500, returned $35,000. Bringing those 1957's to perfection, he held seven track records.

Much of his success came as the result of the engines Dahl was capable of building. One 327 cubic inch engine was rescued from a junked Bake-Rite truck but produced winning results for over two years. Marlin recalls how tough that actually was. "One night at Wisconsin Dells, the throttle stuck. Before I got it shut down, the rpm's had climbed well over eight, and flames were shooting from the exhaust pipes. But it never came apart. It finally did blow one night just after I had won a feature race at Wisconsin Dells. When it came apart, it really came apart. It blew four cylinders out and left the starter dragging in the dirt."

If racing has its tricks now, it did then also. Airplane gas provided a higher octane. "I remember one night, when two-barrel carburetors were the rule, changing to a four-barrel right under everyone's eyes and they never noticed." One summer, the officials at a track locked a chain around the block of his engine until they had time to tear the engine down and look for things that might be illegal. "They never did though, and after half the summer went by, I cut the chain off."

The innovation that led to the funniest story, however, was a trick used to get around the rule that forbade the locking of rear gears. "I used to fill the left rear tire with water. One night at Ladysmith, the axle broke and that big tire must have rolled two miles before it came to a halt. When we finally got it back to the Studebaker Champion we were using as a tow car, it took two men to lift it into the trunk. You should have seen the nose on that Studebaker jump up."

His racing career had many light moments. "One night when we broke down in Black River Falls, Moose Peterson let us sleep in his used car sales building. Already in the building was a myna bird that swore up a storm. Bill Bernhagen started yelling at the bird, trying to get it to shut up. Before it was over, the two had spent the whole night swearing at each other."

15

Grubba

Of his achievements, the greatest are being the Wisconsin champion three times on the dirt at Wausau and winning the National Short Track Championship at Rockford.

AXEL DAHLBERG

Rice Lake champion

Axel Dahlberg is definitely one of the veterans of central Wisconsin racing, having been born in 1937. He raced everything imaginable over a period of more than three decades. He was born in Poskins, Wisconsin, and began his racing career at Rice Lake on the dirt in a 1937 Ford Coupe. "My dad owned a garage. I had turned 16 in March. That summer I went to the races in Rice Lake and the next week I had a car." He would end up winning championships at Emery and Rice Lake. In 1954, he moved up to the modified division, where he ran until 1958.

Dahlberg raced on the dirt until 1973 at such tracks as Superior, Boyceville, Neillsville, Shawano, DePere. He also raced in Stillwater and Proctor, Minn. An early circuit included Stillwater on Wednesday night, Superior on Friday night, Rice Lake on Saturday night, fairs on Sunday afternoon and Proctor on Sunday night. A 15-lap feature at the quarter-mile dirt track at Rice Lake paid about $200 to win.

This early period of racing produced one of Dahlberg's greatest years. In 1957 he campaigned a 1932 Ford coupe with an overhead engine. He collected 57 firsts (not all features), 192 seconds and eight thirds.

In 1958, 1959, and 1960 Axel raced midgets. "Looking back I don't know why I ever drove one; I never felt comfortable," he says. "I was racing at Proctor and I got stupid. Some people were traveling through from out east and they had a midget along that they wanted

17

to sell. I talked Dad into giving me enough money to buy it. We raced a lot of fairgrounds and the tracks were dirty and rough. Tomah, for instance, was so dusty and dirty one evening that they canceled the race. At that time there were a lot of big names campaigning midgets and sprints — Parnelli Jones, Eddie Sachs, Albert George and A.J. Foyt. They were fast and I was trying to run with them. In 1959, there was a 50-lap race at the Minnesota State Fair and Parnelli started 33rd. By the 33rd lap he had lapped the field and he never let off until he broke. That is the kind of racing it was."

One of his worst wrecks occurred in 1958 in Shakopee, Minnesota, during a midget race. "It was in the days when there were no roll bars and if you flipped and lived to tell about it, it was unreal. I flipped five times. The next year a roll bar by your head was mandatory."

On yet another night in Marshfield, a driver hit Dahlberg's stock car and sent him over the guard rail. He hit a tree 15 feet up the trunk and bounced back, landing on the guard rail. When the dust had settled, his car owner came running over to say: "The crowd loved it."

"Maybe they did," Dahlberg responded, "but you aren't going to like the bill!"

Some of the drivers Dahlberg remembers competing against in the 1950's and 1960's include Bud Havel, Don Koepp, Dick Brezmeister, Harold Mueller and Russ Laursen. "Laursen was from Farmington, Minn. It was going to be his last year of racing so he bought an A.J. Foyt sprinter. He got killed in the very last race of the year."

The costs of racing were different in 1963. "I had a 1956 Chevrolet with a 283 in it. The whole car cost $1,800. At one point I bought an engine that had a couple of cracked pistons for $150. I was going to use it a couple of nights and then fix it, but it ran so good I used it until it blew up. I won six features with it and features at places like Rice Lake probably paid $200 to win. One of my better wins that year was at Hibbing, Minn., where I got paid $300."

In 1969 and 1970, Axel raced motorcycles in Colorado. Sunday afternoons found him at Cheyenne, Fort Collins, Greeley and a track outside of Denver. He went over to a friend's shop to visit and ended up buying a dirt bike that had been wrecked. He had an advantage when it came to the standings because anyone over 30 got extra points. Axel was 31. "The first time out I fell a lot. It took one day to learn how to ride. The second time I finished third overall in Class B, which included about 50 riders. I found that it was real strenuous and physical and that there isn't much protection."

In 1972, Dahlberg returned to the Wisconsin dirt tracks and then in 1973 he made the switch to asphalt. In 1974, he drove for Gene Wheeler on the dirt tracks in eastern Wisconsin. In 1975, he drove the sportsman series at LaCrosse and Wisconsin Dells. In the summer of 1976, he competed five nights on a circuit that included West Salem, Wisconsin Dells, Oregon, Plover and Kaukauna. It was an extra thrill when he won his first feature on a Thursday night at Kaukauna.

In 1978, Axel bought a Howe car and returned to the dirt. This time the scene was Iowa and the tracks were Dubuque and Cedar Rapids. One of the biggest thrills of his life would come when he won at Cedar Lake the first night out. It was a 25-lap race and it paid $1,000.

In 1979, Dahlberg switched back to asphalt. Axel dropped from the racing scene from 1982 to 1984 to spend time on business interests, namely, National Energy Systems, a home improvement company that at the time was devoted to solar power. In 1984, his wife talked him back into racing. He had been competing on a limited basis, primarily at Capital Speedway. He was involved in another serious accident at Kaukauna in the summer of 1985. "A car came off the wall and I ran over the front of it and went end for end. A torn rotor cup in my shoulder put me out for the remainder of the 1985 season."

THE EARLY YEARS
Starting out young

Anyone watching Dick Trickle walk will notice a slight limp and probably would presume it is the result of a racing accident. This is a false assumption. When Dick was eight years old, he was playing tag with his brother. Verlin, on the second floor of a house that was under construction. He fell, went through the first floor beams and landed on the concrete in the basement.

When he landed on the basement floor, his hip was shattered. He would pass out in pain. Local doctors transferred him to the University of Wisconsin Hospital. Eventually, the doctors would give up and send him home, presuming he would be an invalid forever. But Dick Trickle was a young boy and young boys don't know they aren't supposed to walk. He stepped on it, limped on it and eventually walked on it.

As the result of the fall, he spent three years in a cast that ran from his waist to his knee on one side and from his waist to his foot on the other side. It didn't slow him down, and he claims to have been the fastest kid in third grade, perhaps a foreboding of things to come. He would later fall out of a tree and shatter the cast, which left the doctor shaking his head and wondering if his patient would ever walk again.

Out of that same childhood, Dick remembers playing BB gun tag. The rules were simple. No head shots. You couldn't use any limbs that got hit. To be shot in the body was to be dead. During the wars of one afternoon, Dick stuck his head around from behind a tree and got shot right between the eyes. Being the oldest player, he called a halt to the action and talked about rules.

When his father was institutionalized with a rare disease, Dick Trickle would taste poverty. At thirteen he was pulling his own weight in the world. He found employment on a farm— milking cows, cleaning barns, filling silos, haying and threshing.

At 15, he began to spend any free time he had at his uncle's blacksmith shop. Occasionally, his uncle would give him a piece of metal that would be stored away in a hope chest for the day he would build a race car.

When he began to race and showed promise as a driver, he was declared too young to race at his home track, Griffith Park. Then, at school, when he was playing basketball, which was a big thing for a boy that age, someone would remember that he was racing in the summer and decide to check out how old he was. Having started school a year older than most and losing a year while in the hospital made him too old to participate. Another obstacle to be overcome.

With this as a background, racing probably didn't look dangerous to him. "From day one, I knew I wanted to be a racer," Trickle says as he looks back. "Gary Giebels had built a 1946 Dodge to race at Stratford, but he was underage and his mother wouldn't sign a release form. We drove all over and finally found my mother, who signed for me. When we got there, I took the car out for hot laps, only to return and tell Gary that it didn't feel right. 'Ah, that is the way they are supposed to feel' was the response. I flipped it during the race. The next week, Gary talked his mother into signing for him, and he flipped it during hot laps. The car wasn't built for racing.

"I knew this was the way for me to go," Dick continues, "so I went and bought back a 1950 Ford that I had owned from a guy for $17.50. Then I bought an engine out of a 1949 Ford from a guy who had been beating me in the streets for $32.50 and went racing."

The first evening he started in the last position and worked his way up to third before the leaders spun out in front of him. One of the cars smashed the left side of his racer, and Trickle's crew later installed a grader blade on that side to protect their rookie driver.

The place of initiation was Stratford. The veterans were Don Ruder, Jere O'Day, Ray Hoffman, Red Nichols, Jerry Bredl, Augie Winkleman, Dave Marcis, and Marlin Walbeck. "We were just dummies starting out," Trickle recalls. "Marlin Walbeck was really smooth. He was ahead of everyone when it came to setting cars up."

Marv Marzofka's axe-hewn Studebaker was shoved over a sand pile by a big Buick, but he won the second race he entered when he saw the Buick looming in the background again. Orv Buelow slammed into the plank retaining wall, watched the sand slowly seep between the boards on his crumpled hood and wondered what the repair cost would be.

Tom Reffner started racing at Stratford in 1959 and doesn't remember seeing anything because of the dust. Welding specks on his glasses probably prohibited Jimmy Back from witnessing any of the horrors of his first race.

Nineteen-fifty-nine would be the year that Sam Bartus opened the first paved track in the area, Griffith Park. Soon Adams-Friendship was paved, then Tomah-Sparta, and a whole circuit developed. It was an era of an A and B feature.

"Everybody wanted to be a hot dog," Marzofka recalls. It was an era when body styles dictated whether you were in the feature or semi, and it was possible to bring two cars and race all night. In the early days, feature cars had 1957 or newer sheet metal. All older body styles were in the semi-feature, regardless of how they timed in. Some drivers like Homer Spink chose to move up to the feature. Some were forced. When Back proved untouchable in a 1953 Mercury, the opposition told him that if he came back with a wheelbarrow the next year

Dick Trickle (99) battles Steve Burgess (12) and Dave Watson (37) for the lead at LaCrosse.

he was going into the feature."

Above all, it was an era of footloose fun, and a lot of the excitement emanated from a shop in Vesper, Wisconsin, where Jimmy Back and Tom Reffner were partners. It was the home of the dreaded child-chasing Silo Monster, the Garage Cat that fought Orv Buelow tooth and nail, and Rufus, the antifreeze-drinking dog. It was the home of many midnight inventions and pranks, such as the night Reffner went to steal some of the neighbor's apples and had Back drive into the yard and shine a spotlight on him while he was in the tree.

Being at the track didn't change things. At that time, Reffner and Back hauled their race cars on a truck and trailer, and their loading technique kept a crowd of on-lookers around long after the races were over. After picking up their winnings and a session at the beer tent, the ritual began. The team would get out a set of planks and run the first car on the trailer. Then the planks were moved and the first car was run up on the truck. Flying planks caused the timid to watch from a distance. A climax was reached at Griffith Park when Back failed to wait for the planks to be shifted around and wedged the stock car between the truck and trailer. According to Reffner, "it took every last onlooker to get it out of there."

It was a time of fun between races. Jimmy Back's birthday party was at Tom's Tavern in Wyeville. Tom Reffner, Marv Marzofka, Dean Spohn and others had gathered there after the races at Tomah-Sparta, and it became known that it was Back's birthday. He was soon on the floor getting a spanking, a fate that befell any driver whose birthday became known thereafter. If there was a long gap between dates, it was simply declared to be someone's birthday so festivities could continue.

It was a time when the cars were inexpensive, everyone raced and a car would be rolled over to collect a case of beer. "There was a 12-foot drop off the back straight at Adams-Friendship," Don Ruder remembers, "and I sailed off it several times." Marv Marzofka saw a car sail off that same bank and glide, as if suspended by the mercy and finger of God, over a huge line pole that had been cut off a few feet from the ground. Moose Peterson rolled a 1956 Chevy in the fourth turn and crashed to the roof when he released the seat belt holding his suspended body. An old Ford coupe rolled down the front straight, the body going one way and the frame another.

Dick Trickle, who now feels an immaculate car is desirable, says of his own car raced in those days: "I would have washed it, but I didn't want to cut my hands!" Howard Johnson, Dells promoter, offered him money to paint it. Marlin Walbeck did paint the hood an ugly green that Trickle left on for all to see

It was an era in which Roho, Lyle Nabbefeldt's constant companion in the 1933 Chevy Chicken Coupe, felt right at home. The grizzly, greasy rooster could be seen on a nightly basis, digging his hackles into the roll cage beside Lyle, especially after an end-for-end flip at Golden Sands. "When I walked back, I found my lighter where I flipped the first time, my cigarettes where flipped the second and Roho where I landed the third time. He hung on for dear life after that."

After the races, the "Legendary Leghorn" took his customary perch on the edge of a bar and indulged in peanuts and beer offered by the drivers. As he got drunk, he would bury his beak right up to his eyes in the shot glass of beer and then settle down on his haunches and go to sleep.

All went well until Francis Kelly took him to Tomah and his Tepee Supper Club for some rest and relaxation. It was there that they switched his drink to vodka and instead of settling down on the bar when he had imbibed too much, Roho would fall over backwards and land bottom-up on the floor. Roho survived the vigors of racing, only to die of pneumonia.

It was a time that came to an end. Tom Reffner can look back after an evening of stories and ask, "How come we don't have time for all this stuff anymore?"

In 1966, Dick Trickle won the National Short Track title at Rockford. It was the first time that he had been out of central Wisconsin. It was a turning point in what he expected of himself and what his fans expected of him. "I looked at all those drivers gathered from around the country and said, 'You are as fast as any of them.' Soon, I began to travel and my fans began to expect that win. There are times when I am satisfied with a second or third, but they aren't." Out of all the dust and banging around, there began to appear a group of professional drivers.

1967

Shoes in his finest hour

When the 1967 season opened on a Thursday evening in Wausau, Dick Trickle beat Marlin Walbeck by a fender; but when the season ended, Shoes Walbeck would bask in the glow of his greatest victory.

Running on Thursday evening put the State Park Speedway in direct competition with Griffith Park in Wisconsin Rapids and, eventually, Sam Bartus handed over the Wausau reins to John Murgatroyd, who made Wausau the first stop on the circuit by switching to Tuesday evenings. When the track reopened under new management on July 18, Trickle and Walbeck were still dueling for top spot in the feature, but it was Rich Somers who brought the crowd to its feet by putting in a disappearing act over the bank in the third turn.

In August, Ken Pankratz, veteran T-Bird driver, gave lessons to new gladiators and held off Trickle, Jim Back and Dave Field. Lyle Nabbefeldt had his car burst into flames after crashing into two cars that had spun in front of him. Marlin Walbeck won the finale with Nabbefeldt finishing second.

From Wausau, the racers hauled to the Speedbowl in north LaCrosse. Although its two feet of sand had given way to asphalt, the track still had character. It was dimly lit. It had a pool of water in the center that turned into a lake after several rainfalls. It had trees in the pit area that served as cheap seats for spectators and a haven to mosquitoes as big as blue jays. Winners varied — Nelson Drinkwine, Everett Fox and Gordy Clay were but a few. On August 2, Les Katzner won an accident-spiced feature in which he had been involved in a five-car wreck that Dick Trickle triggered by trying to pass Katzner for the lead.

Thursday night brought the traveling band of racers roaring down the ramp to do battle at Griffith Park. On May 21, all of the thrills and chills weren't provided by the 74 cars that gathered. Homer Spink of Baraboo, driving in feature events for the first year, beat Tom Reffner and Dave Fields. Roger Olson caused some thrills by flipping his car for the second time in two weeks. But the real chills were provided by the temperature, which dipped to twenty-one degrees.

In June, the track was resurfaced and widened, which led to continuous assaults on the track record as the summer progressed. On the first night, Dick Trickle blew the wrapping off the new pavement with a 13.95 and then went on to an easy feature victory, while Homer Spink and Gordie Clay fought it out for second. The very next week, Marv Marzofka rolled off the hill and dropped the record to 13.94. Ron Beyers eliminated that in a maroon Chevelle with a 13.86. Then, Dick Trickle, as time trials were about to close, snapped his title back with a 13.76. Another week went by, and Marlin Walbeck broke across the timing light with a 13.68.

But the hot dogs didn't do all the winning. Homer Spink held off Dick Trickle for 20 laps to win one evening. On another evening, Spink, Marzofka, Back, Trickle and Pankratz finished under a blanket, with Homer getting his bumper across the line first. Everett Fox did a tailspin and took five cars with him one evening, but then came back the next Thursday night to start in front and stay there till the checkered dropped. However, the finale belonged to Trickle and it was his 25th feature win of the year.

Friday night found everyone on the road again. Oregon's quarter-mile, where Ed Hume reigned supreme in a 1959 Plymouth with a 426 hemi, was raided occasionally, but most drivers concentrated their efforts on the drag-strip oval at Tomah-Sparta.

Hume broke Ken Pankratz's record with a 13.93 early in May and then settled down to weekly struggles that were, for the most part, waged against Bill Retallick, Don and Rudy Bandt, and Richie Bickle. Hume was hit

and spun out on lap ten in a June race. Demonstrating the Plymouth's brutish power, he started from the back and roared through the opposition to win the 50-lapper. June also saw Bill Retallick giving lessons in durability, as he survived a seventy-five-mile-per-hour crash and still won the feature.

In late July, Ken Pankratz towed his 1960 T-Bird down and blew everyone off. Marlin Walbeck then swept down with his 1964 Chevelle 427 and set fast time with a 13.90 but

"Big John" Bottcher helped build many racers in the Wisconsin Rapids area during the early days.

couldn't get by Retallick at the finish, even though he pulled up on the outside of Retallick several times. In August, Dave Field drove his bedraggled but fast 1959 Ford convertible to a 13.87. Bob Beattie of Edgerton won the final race twice. The scorer forgot that the feature had been extended to 50 laps. An excited Beattie, who was leading at that point, jumped out of his car in front of the judges stand, and after a heated discussion jumped back in and drove on to victory.

At LaCrosse, the Wisconsin Rapids crowd had it their own way. Homer Spink drove his 1961 Ford to victory one evening when Trickle, Marzofka, Walbeck, and Nelson Drinkwine almost eliminated each other, but the consistent winners were Trickle, Marzofka and Field. On a night that saw Lyle Nabbefeldt set fast time in his 1933 Chevy coupe, Dewey Moore did a triple barrel roll in the hobby division. July 28 was a night Louie Vetrone remembered, as he won the second heat and began a tremendous comeback from a broken neck suffered in a racing accident that had kept him sidelined since 1963.

In 1967, the Dells Motor Speedway was a quarter-mile track that got visited on Saturday night. Les Katzner and Marv Marzofka opened the summer program with a wheel-to-wheel duel that finally went to Katzner. Dick Collins rolled his hobby stocker to end the evening. Later in the year, Les Katzner saw his attempts to pass Dave Fields for the lead come to an end when he lost control of his 1957 Chevy in turn four and did a complete rollover that brought him to rest in front of the judges stand and a pale announcer, Don Ruder.

John McFaul held off Tom Reffner and Bud Schroeder on a night when Jeff DeLapp went off the north bank and Dale Walworth and Ed Dorl traded paint.

Dick Trickle, in a 1967 Mercury, edged Marzofka on a night of racing that was so violent the hobbies were postponed after Clarence Roberts of Wisconsin Rapids rolled three-and-a-half times and ended up on his roof. In the same accident, Oliver Leege of Portage snap-rolled with such force that one of his shoes was torn off and pitched into oblivion.

Trickle's name ended up on top at the Dells often that summer. But on a July night that saw a record crowd of 3,083, Tom Reffner won after Trickle blew a tire. In the final race, Walbeck got trapped behind some slower cars on the inside, while Trickle slipped by on the outside and collected the checkered and $448.

It took some waiting, but Golden Sands, near Wisconsin Rapids, opened on Sunday, May 30. Dick Trickle toured the new third-mile oval in his 1966 Comet with a fast 13.69. Rich Somers grabbed the lead from Dave

Marcis to win the fast heat. Lyle Nabbefeldt won the semi and third heat. Trickle won the feature event.

Walbeck finished second to Tom Reffner in a special Memorial Day 50. Trickle replaced his clutch before the feature and then blew his engine on lap 20.

Racing was close all summer. Back got beside Somers and took a feature by a fender length. Walbeck couldn't get around Trickle. Trickle held off Somers. Beyers tried to hold off Trickle as he stormed from last place to first. Gordy Clay repaired his 1963 Ford and won but was constantly pressured by Somers. Jere O'Day finished second to Fields in a 40-lap mid-season race.

There were some wrecks. Bill Wirtz was dazed when he crashed into the retaining wall at full power. Howie Chamberlain did two quick end-over-end flips, bounced sideways and then took two more rolls. In a feat equal to anything the Wright Brothers ever accomplished, Albert Getzloff took flight and rolled several times. Dave Field saw his chances of winning a feature go up in flames as he was sitting on the starting line. Trickle had a fire coming to the races that burned most of his car.

In 1967, there was only one championship race and it was held in Rockford at the close of the season. To win it was to be king. For years it had eluded Marlin Walbeck. In the fall of 1967, he prepared as he never had before. As the gas drained from the drum in the trunk, the lightened car ran smoother and smoother. At the end of the race, the crowd swept out of the stands and stood around to congratulate him. Dick Trickle might have won the year before, but the old master had put it all together for his final and greatest victory. "Shoes" smiled as he leaned against the car. A future generation could now take over.

1968
Year of the mad dog racer

"Eventually." Dick Trickle said, "twenty or thirty professional drivers would rise to the top, but in the early days of my racing, everyone had a car and there was a lot of crashing and banging."

If one doubts Trickle's words, all one has to do is return to 1968 and the North LaCrosse Speedbowl. Dick Trickle won the opening feature in quiet enough fashion, but in the third heat there was a spectacular crash in which Ed Viner of LaCrosse flipped his car on its top, tearing off both trunk and roof. Fortunately, the roll bar held and Ed escaped with a few scratches and a bit dusty.

The next night out, Larry Baumel, the only person to ever race a station wagon, beat Dave Marcis, who had returned to Wisconsin after driving in the Daytona 500. Again, spin-outs were numerous as a result of high winds blowing sand on the track. Howard Allen and Don Grant provided early thrills by rolling their cars at the close of warm-ups. During the second heat, Howard Vinson came to rest in the infield after rolling over twice.

The first race date in June, Homer Spink survived a five-car crash in the feature to win. Nine out of the 17 cars entered in the hobby feature were demolished, and eight cars never made it to the finish line in the consolation race.

Later in June, five days of rain made it necessary to pump the infield, in which Homer Spink almost drowned, but it still looked like a swimming pool as the races started. Dick Trickle took the lead from Everett Fox on the 13th lap and went on to win but only after Dick Rogers and Loren Iverson had sailed over the sand bank in the northeast turn and came to rest with only the trunks of their cars visible.

The hobby stockers made July a field day for tow trucks. On July 24, five collided and one became airborne, vanishing into the trees surrounding the track. On July 31, Leon Trickle rolled four times and ended up out in the trees with his hood folded and trunk gone.

But it wasn't just the little guys who kept the weeds from growing on the sand banks. Dick Trickle, who won a good number of features at La Crosse and was on his way to being USAC rookie of the year, watched one race from the sand bank after trying to avoid a spinning Lyle Nabbefeldt. On lap 15 of the final race of the year, Tom Reffner went up in the air and over the sand bank in the northeast corner.

At Tomah-Sparta, the Friday night stop on the circuit, Tom Reffner was busy pursuing Rich Somers out in the weeds off turn three. Marlin Walbeck brought an axe and sent a ripple of laughter through the crowd as he cut down a tree that he had collided with at a previous race. Don Stoeckly and Denny Jensen met head-on in a hobby race and were then administered the *coup de grace* by Roy Malette, who roared into the disabled vehicles. Pete Mahlum spiced up late model racing with a metal-tearing rollover. As Bobby Allison has said. "You know you are in trouble when you are sailing along and the crowd is upside down and running for cover."

On the serious side, Dale Walworth rose from the cranberry bogs of Warrens and surprised everyone by winning the opener at Tomah-Sparta. Everett Fox proved that the venerable 1957 Chevy had not died by beating Billy Wirtz and Larry Baumel in one feature and holding off the challenges of Dick Trickle in another. Dick Trickle came from the back of the pack in a Fourth of July special to finish ahead of Fox, Gordy Clay and Dave Marcis. "The Ridge Runner," Marv Marzofka, lived up to his nickname and slipped by Larry Rezen to win a feature that left Dick Schultz of Wausau and Trickle battling for third.

At Wisconsin Dells, Dick Walkush shortened his season to one race when he flipped and totally destroyed his racer in the semi-feature on the opening Saturday night. Fritz Bishofberger proved that Dick Trickle's Mercury Comet still had plenty of life left in it, as he collected the major portion of the $2.500 being offered to the 100 cars present, by edging Marlin Walbeck in the feature. Bob Zynda should have won the semi-feature, but in his haste to got to the checkered flag, he spun out and gave the victory to Larry Baumel.

At the July Fourth special, 102 cars showed up to provide the action, and every race was red-flagged except the feature. Les Grant brought the wreckers out and the kids to the fence, as he flipped four times.

Later in the season, Fritz Bishofberger locked horns with the pine trees off the north end of the track and Dale Walworth brought the crowd to its feet, as he flipped end-for-end, beginning at pit road and disappearing behind the bank on turn three. The Indian that was painted on the side of Walworth's car got his scalp tickled that night.

Post-race attitudinal adjustment sessions at the beer stand were often a necessity as tempers flared. Billy Wirtz and John McNamara stood nose-to-nose discussing racing etiquette one evening after Wirtz's car came to a rest on the hood of McNamara's on the front straight.

Among the survivors, Marlin Walbeck established a new track record with his 1966 Chevelle when he dropped his own mark from 13.13 to 13.11. The heavyweights — Marzofka, Back, Reffner, Field — won their share of features, but the lesser knowns also picked up a checkered or two. Mike Brown of Wisconsin Dells beat Dick Severson of LaCrosse. George Thornton of Endeavor warded off the challenges of Walbeck and Dick Schultz. In the semi-features, Walworth, Ray Hoffman, Del Kemnitz and Bud Schroeder kept the opposition scrambling.

The deer that rest in the woods at the north edge of Golden Sands Speedway must have wondered if there was a full moon every Sunday night. Cars, and crop dusters over local potato fields, were taking to the air and shaking their peaceful retreat.

Not only the deer, but flagman Minnow Moll found that it wasn't too safe near the edge of the track. Earl Sharping got Minnow's flag rack and almost Minnow on one occasion. On another, a car slammed into a sand bank before him, and Minnow escaped being decapitated by a flying windshield when he tripped while trying to escape and fell to the ground.

Morrie Piotrowski proved that he could fly higher than a crop duster when he lost a front spindle, but his landing against a brick wall was a lot less gracious.

Pat Griffin spun on the second lap of a semi-feature and took three cars with him into the sand piles. On the restart, Pat again proved that only planes should fly, as he flew over a 12-foot bank and lost all four wheels on his car upon impact.

Jimmy Back won a feature in his 1962 Ford that had only six cars finish. On lap one, Trickle, Fox and Spink tangled, with Spink flying over an embankment and flipping

If the deer weren't safe, the mosquitoes also suffered from smoke inhalation at Golden Sands in the summer of 1968. What the frost hadn't already killed, Dick Trickle put to rest in the final race of the season. A first-lap wreck pushed the fan through the radiator on number 99 and Trickle retired to the pits. On lap 16, Trickle, in his determined fashion, was back on the track running without a fan belt. The smoking engine finally froze on lap 38.

When they were on the track, Marv Marzofka dominated the early season in a 1967 Ford. June was Ford
month, and on one occasion the first four finishers were
Fords. Tom Reffner, in a 1967 Ford, beat Gordy Clay,
who was driving a 1966 Ford. Homer Spink finished third
in a 1967 Ford, with Dick Trickle's 1967 Fairlane right
on his bumper. June was also Reffner's month, as he
won a close battle with Trickle and then started the
new month with a 75-lap victory on the Fourth of July.

Jimmy Back was the hottest driver on the circuit in
the month of August and at Golden Sands he came from
the back to win the 75-lap mid-season championships.
He won another weekly show and then, in a special 45-
lap feature, came from the back to take the lead from
Dave Field on lap 40.

Ron Beyers won a feature. Dave Marcis won a feature. Mike Brown won the 75-lap Memorial Day feature
in a 1966 Chevelle that he purchased from Lyle
Nabbefeldt. In the semi-features, Robert Mackesy,
Sonny Immerfall, Bill Wirtz, John Brevick and Dick
Severson were but a few who paused for applause in
front of the crowd.

But when it came down to the 100-lap state championship, Marlin Walbeck was the victor. Jimmy Back tried
to take the lead on the curves, but his efforts fell short.

Kaukauna, then the only paved, high-banked half-
mile, celebrated its grand opening on June 2, 1968. Dick
Trickle dominated the action there and finished the
season by winning a 100-lapper.

The offering of a trophy brings out the mad dog in
any racer. Looking back at 1968 and the number of flips
and wrecks that occurred, there must have been an
abundance of trophy nights.

JIMMY BACK
Do or die
and let the parts fly

To know Jimmy Back was to know a legend in the making. What Willie Nelson is to the music world, Jimmy Back is to central Wisconsin racing.

He began his career in 1960 in a 1952 Mercury. It started out with two partners and Back as the welder but it wasn't long before the others discovered girls and Back was the sole owner and driver of the car.

His philosophy, on and off the track, always was "do or die and let the parts fly." When one of his early race cars was destroyed, he went home and cut up the family car. The next Sunday morning, he and his wife and six kids headed for church in a pickup truck.

When he had the equipment, Jim was untouchable. Tom Reffner, who drove for him in the early years, said, "When Back is running, nobody can touch him."

If anything slowed him down it was an accident that occurred on the way to a race rather than at the race track. Traveling on Highway 13 west of Pittsville, he stopped to let oncoming traffic go by before turning onto County X. A semi hit him from behind, destroyed his race car and left him with serious neck and back injuries. He would race no more in 1986 and would struggle through the 1987 season. Even so, he won features at Wausau and West Salem and at West Salem collected a bounty for beating Tom Reffner, who was in the process of having a fine year.

When Back began his career in the early 1960's, a

feature car was one with 1957 or newer sheet metal. All older cars went in the semi-feature without regard for how fast they timed in at the beginning of the evening. Back had a 1953 Mercury that was unbeatable. Then a simple body style change permitted him to call it a 1954 Mercury and enabled him to use even stronger motors. The results were devastating and track officials reacted strongly. "At the end of the season," Jim says, "they told me that even if I came back with a wheelbarrow the next year I was going in the feature."

During these years, Back had two cars. The second was driven by Tom Reffner. They hauled the cars to the various tracks with a truck and a trailer and the loading of the cars after the races was often more exciting than the races.

From the beginning of his career, Back operated out of his own shop in a rural area near Vesper, Wisconsin. He and his wife, Cyrilla, lived in a white house nearby and watched as their nine children grew up and left home. It was a special time for racing in central Wisconsin. There was always room for fun.

When the children were young the story of the "Silo Monster" was developed by Jim and Tom Reffner and whoever might be working on a car at Jim's shop on a particular evening. The Silo Monster lived, naturally enough, in a silo on the farm. The stories grew as it drew closer to bedtime for Jim's children. Tom Reffner claimed to have seen it. Fearful, running children dashed from the shop to the house in the darkness of evening pursued by terrible sounds that, on closer investigation, might have been found to be coming from the shop rather than the silo.

The shop was guarded by Rufus the dog, who was known to get high on antifreeze. It also contained "Garage Cat." Garage Cat hated Orv Buelow, a race car driver, and waited for an opportunity to strike out at him. The occasion came one day when Orv and five others were carrying an engine across the shop. Sensing that Orv could not let go of the engine, Garage Cat

Jimmy Back waits for an introduction at Wisconsin Dells.

jumped on Orv's leg and bit and scratched him as hard as he could. Then he ran out the door and disappeared for two weeks.

Back had a knack for falling asleep instantly, whether he was eating or standing up. There is a story about him stopping at an all-night restaurant in Tomah and ordering meatballs and spaghetti. He fell sound asleep in the course of eating the meal and dropped face down in the dish. His wife, Cyrilla, assured everyone around that he was all right, although some wondered how he was managing to breathe.

On a trip home from racing in Elko, Minnesota, Tom Reffner's crew came up on Back's hauler pulled off to the side of the road. There was Jim standing alongside the truck sleeping with a gas can in his hands, the filler spout stuck in the side of the truck. He had fallen asleep while pouring gas in the disabled vehicle.

Those who tried to keep up with Back were often left wondering. Ron Petrowski, a member of his crew at one time said, "It must be the sleep that makes me sick. I always feel pretty good when I go to bed." It has been said that Jim enjoys taking others out for the whole evening knowing that he can go home and sleep while they must go straight to work.

Marv Marzofka once tried to summarize the scene: "Jimmy Back is probably the best philosopher in the world. The problem is nobody can remember what he said in the morning. The last thing you remember is Back standing there in a perilous lean, making a half stab at your belt buckle with his cigarette hand, while thoughts begin with a name and wander off into nowhere: 'Now Dick... Now Tom ...' "

After Back quit smoking, he still knew how to philosophize. "You know how he kind of puts his head back and rubs his neck with his hand," Steve Carlson said after a post-race gathering. "I had bumped him during a race that evening and then he had bumped me back. At first it was 'Some driver.' Then it was 'A certain driver ...'. It ended up with 'The next time you do that ....'"

Nelson Drinkwine knows about that "next time." Once at Golden Sands, with five laps to go, Drinkwine and Back, going for the lead, collided. Back continued to lead but Drinkwine went off the track and had to start over from the rear. By the last lap, Drinkwine was again challenging Back for the lead. They collided again on the front straight, but this time Back went off the outer edge of the track and Drinkwine won the feature. Back just waited with the front of his car still pointed at the crowd. As Drinkwine stopped to pick up the checkered flag, Back's car rolled — with some help from the motor — down the incline of the track and into the side of Drinkwine's car. The car that Drinkwine was driving belonged to Dick Trickle and, when it got back to the shop, crewman John Botcher would say, "I kicked on it and hammered on it for a week before it was straight."

Another Botcher-Back incident occurred in the days when both Trickle and Back were transporting two cars apiece to the track with trucks and trailers. Back's truck broke down one evening on the way to Wausau and Trickle offered to give him a tow. They made it to the races and, when the program was over, Back got a 100-mph tow home. At one point on that return trip, they passed a highway patrolman and Back let his rig get within inches of Trickle's so that the officer couldn't see the tow chain. Back remembered the low flight and returned the favor one evening on a return trip from Capital Speedway in Madison. When Trickle's hauler broke down, Jim towed it through an intersection in such a fashion that it left the disabled vehicle out in oncoming traffic during a red light with Botcher at the wheel.

In the early days, Jim was also known as an innovator. Marv Marzofka summed it up: "Jim is a man full of ideas. First he tinkered with engines. He drilled holes in the skirts of pistons to get more power. The car flew, but the engine didn't last. Then Jim began to work on suspension. He had a twin I-beam in his 1956 Ford. The car was so low that he couldn't use the normal drag link steering set up, so he devised a roller chain system that turned the front wheels independently from under the dash. From suspension, he went to aerodynamics."

As a result of his welding, Back's glasses have often been a point of conversation as they are filled with welding specks. Some have suggested that the peaks in his career have occurred whenever he has new glasses and can see clearly. Back himself jokes about it and says that once, when he got new glasses, his times at LaCrosse dropped seven-tenths of a second. Sometimes, when he gets new glasses, he claims he can read numbers in the parts book that he didn't even know were there before. He also claims to have been frightened to death when a moth crawled out of one of those parts books and he, catching a glimpse of it through new bifocals, thought he was being attacked by a monster.

Still, he is a very skilled driver. One evening at Wisconsin Dells, a steering arm snapped as Jim was going down the front straight. The car traveled along the wall, showering sparks everywhere. When it was all over, only the back bumper had suffered damage. Back had saved the car by feathering the gas pedal until the car came to a halt.

Jim is also one to see the humor in an event. At Wausau, he once crawled out of a stack of wrecked cars on the front straight and said, "And we are supposed to be professionals!"

One of Jim's most violent wrecks happened on the dirt at Wausau's State Fair Park. Back flipped his Camaro end-for-end. A member of Dick Trickle's crew ran over and, spotting a dark fluid on Jim's uniform, thought he had killed himself. The dark fluid turned out to be oil, but this time Jim wasn't talking. He had bit his tongue during the roll over.

Some of the best years in Back's long career were a span in the mid-1970's when he and Robert Holmes fielded a series of Bemco chassied Camaros. In 1973, the team won 17 features. In 1974, they won 19 features. Back would hold track records at four different tracks.

When drivers are winning, they travel, and Jim Back was no exception. Once, on a return trip from I-70 Speedway in Odessa, Missouri, Jim was sound asleep in the compartment behind the seat of the truck as the driver, Coyote, was sailing along a country road shortcut. Coyote dozed off just as they were coming to a T intersection. *R-r-rump* went the tires as they sped over the first warning ridges. Back woke up and looked at the sleeping Coyote. "Coyote," he yelled, "you better do something!" Coyote slept on. *R-r-rump* went the speeding tires again. "Coyote," Back yelled again. "You better do something!" Now Back was down in the seat shaking Coyote. The end of the road was coming up very fast. There was just enough time to take a look off the end of the road, where a farmer had come to a stop on his tractor. With a frozen face, he watched the hauler approach at 80 mph. "Coyote," Back yelled a final time. Coyote came to, slammed his foot on the brake pedal, and turned a hard right. "I think the padlocks on the side of the truck must have scraped on the ground as we made the corner," said Back.

When Back and Holmes parted company, Back went back to building and fielding his own cars, known as Bac-Kars. Those on the circuit who have purchased them are known as Backie's fleet. In the 1980's a change began to take place. While his cars were often bent and battered before, when he picked up Twin Grove Manufacturing and later Ho-Chunk Bingo as his sponsors, his cars took on an immaculate appearance. In fact, they have been some of the finest looking cars on the circuit. In 1985, he was the CWRA point champion. Only a serious highway accident kept him from being in true form, but in 1987, he was again third in the points.

While he continued to win, there were always the incidents away from the track that claimed attention. A final one is the famous bus ride to and from LaCrosse Speedway. It was so memorable that driver Jim Dumdee, a member of Backie's fleet, thought it fitting to have a T-shirt made up marking the occasion. The trip began with the fuel pump breaking in the bus that was being used as a hauler on the way to LaCrosse. This caused gas to be pumped into the motor, ruining it. Promotor Larry Wehrs came to the rescue by sending his wrecker out to tow the bus to the track.

At the track, the race car was destroyed in a race. It was pushed back into the bus, which was hitched to Joe Krzykowski's hauler for the trip home.

As they were traveling down Highway 131, the hauler braked sharply for a deer. Unfortunately, the bus had vacuum brakes, which were good for one pump without the engine running. The one pump did not keep the bus from shortening itself up against the hauler. With the front fenders pushed into the tires, the bus became impossible to steer and left Jim yelling at the bus driver, "Don't spin the bus out!'"

In the meantime, the impact sent the toolbox sliding forward into the door well with Jim's son, Wayne, close behind. The impact also caused the stock car to break its chains and knock the partition between it and the crew down. Joe Krzykowski, who was laying in a

Jimmy Back was best known for glasses covered with welding specks. He also was known for experiments such as drilling holes in the skirts of pistons.

bunk, ended up with his arm stuck right through the partition. It brought to a halt a great card game that was going on at the time.

After the dust settled, someone suggested going back and looking for the deer, but the mosquitoes were so fierce the project was abandoned. "The mosquitoes were so bad, we think the deer jumped in front of the hauler to commit suicide and get away from them," commented a crew member.

While it may be apocryphal, one last story deserves telling. It dates from the early days of Jim's shop. Orv Buelow does the telling: "Earlier in the evening, Tom Reffner and Jim wouldn't let me cut up a certain piece of metal to use on my racer. But then after the work was done for the evening, they got talking about attaching car springs to their feet and surprising everyone in the pits some night by jumping over their cars. It didn't take long and they had the metal cut up and welded to the top of some coil springs. Strapping the invention to their feet, they proceeded to jump off the shop roof. It worked, but instead of slowing down you went faster and faster until you fell on your face."

Jimmy Back kept bouncing along, becoming more of a legend each day.

1969
Bartus wows them

Time was quickly passing by the quarter-mile bull ring of central Wisconsin. Kaukauna was the first half-mile paved facility to be built but, within a year, Sam Bartus had countered by tearing up his old quarter-mile on the outskirts of Oregon and building Capital Super Speedway. In the inaugural race, Marv Marzofka was leading by a half lap and seemed well on his way to victory when he blew a tire, giving way to a three-car race to the finish by Ramo Stott, Jim Back, and Tom Reffner. Back and Reffner shot past Ramo's Plymouth Hemi, but then all collided and went into the infield. Stott recovered first and took the win.

In the second race program, Dick Trickle demonstrated his mechanical skills by completely rebuilding the front of his car after crashing in the heat race. Then, minus hood and fenders, he drove his 1966 Ford to a narrow victory over Marzofka and Back. Bert Knutson became one of the first to experience what the results of a high-speed crash at Capital would be like when he flipped his car over the sand bank, which would later be replaced by a retaining wall, and destroyed it.

Jimmy Back discovered one of the early, unexpected hazards of racing at Capital Speedway, "Joe Shear hit me and I got sideways. There was a concrete culvert end hidden in the infield grass. I couldn't believe it! At first I didn't know what hit me. You expect to get hit from the front, or the rear, or the side, but how many

Birdie Gau often gave out the trophies during the 1960's at Dells Speedway.

drivers get hit from the bottom?" It broke the motor mounts, ripped off the oil lines and bent the frame.

Back would also establish himself as the track's first points champion as the summer went by, followed by Tom Reffner and Marv Marzofka. In June, Back took the lead on the last lap of the feature and finished ahead of Marzofka. Trickle beat Back in a bumper-to-bumper duel.

Back beat Marzofka in July in a race that saw Bill Retallick lose control, crash into the front straight wall, and slide the full length of the track. Back started August by setting fast time and winning the feature. Johnny Ziegler captured the mid-season championship and then came back on Friday night to take his second feature in twenty-four hours. That same Friday night saw Marzofka collecting a $200 bounty for cracking the 20-second qualifying barrier. Back capped off the season by winning the 75-lap championship. A new era of super-speedways had been inaugurated.

In 1969, most of the race drivers stepped out of the new-found speeds at Oregon and back into the snail's pace offered by the quarter-mile at Wisconsin Dells. Dick Trickle won the opener. In the second event of the year, Marzofka held off "Jumping Jimmy" Back in the feature, and Del Kemnitz narrowly beat Tom Jensen in the semi-feature. The next time around, Jensen got his first feature win in a 1960 Ford by holding off Back and his 1967 Ford.

In the first race of August, Marv Marzofka, in a 1967 Ford, edged out Fritz Bishofberger. Ed Nichols of Portage followed them across the line. The excitement wasn't limited to the feature. Len Swalheim rolled his 1965 Studebaker in the semi-feature. The season closed with a variety of winners: Lyle Nabbefeldt, Homer Spink, Kato Thiesen, Johnny Ziegler, Del Kemnitz, and Dave Fields.

North LaCrosse began its season running on the same night as Wisconsin Dells. Dale Walworth set fast time opening night and then finished third in the feature, behind Larry Anderson and Don Grant. In the second program, Ralph Bakewell lost an early lead and finished second to John Stott. In an attempt to draw more competitors, the speedway switched to Wednesday evenings. Marv Marzofka benefited the most from the change, as he took the majority of the features during the remainder of the season. His string of victories was interrupted by Tom Schaller, Tom Jensen, Jim Sauter and John Brevick, who won the final event of the season by escaping a 10-car crash.

The original half-mile track in Wisconsin, Kaukauna, ran on Thursday night, and the season began as it had left off, with Dick Trickle dominating the feature events. As the season progressed, more and more of the central Wisconsin drivers began the trek to Kaukauna, and Trickle found the going more difficult. Marlin Walbeck, Jim Back, Tom Reffner, and Marv Marzofka were soon taking home checkered flags from the speedway.

The season opened with Nelson Drinkwine surviving three crashes to win the feature. The next week, Trickle returned to the circuit from his USAC ventures to win the feature for himself. It was an evening that saw Earl Sharping knock the back right off of Willie Rhinewand's car. The crowd sang happy birthday to

Marv Marzofka, and Jim Back set a track record in his 1968 Ford.

Marv Marzofka almost stopped the string of victories by Trickle's car when he passed Trickle on lap 37 of a 75-lap Memorial Day special and kept his 1967 Comet out in front until lap 68, when Trickle passed him back and went on to win the event. Dale Walworth, in his 1958 Ford, beat Sonny Immerfall, who was driving a 1956 Comet, in the semi-feature.

Another week went by, and this time Trickle stopped on his way home from Kaukauna to win still another feature. This time, he roared past Bill Wirtz on lap 15 to take the lead and went on to win by two laps.

The next week, Marv Marzofka set fast time, but it was Trickle who won the feature. Roy Gau made it a partial drive in darkness when he hit a light pole previous to the feature and took out five lights. While Trickle was dominating the late models, Fluff Furo was throwing his weight around in the hobbies and won his fifth straight on the same evening.

Trickle won again on June 15, and then on the Fourth of July, Marv Marzofka returned from an afternoon victory at Capital Speedway to beat out Tom Reffner for the second time that day and win $300 from a purse of $3,300.

It was then that lightning struck in the form of a track boycott. The central Wisconsin drivers' organization, angered by the lack of safety equipment and insurance, boycotted Golden Sands. After negotiating with John Murgatroyd, Howard Johnson leased Griffith Park and reopened it on July 13. The battle lines were clearly formed. On August 11, Sam Bartus announced that he had severed all connections with the CWRA and would reopen Golden Sands. Any driver or crew was welcome to return with the exception of Dave Field and Clem Droste, whom he labeled instigators. The season ended without compromise.

<u>J.J. SMITH</u>

Fooling around leads to racing career

After more than three decades as one of north-eastern Wisconsin's top drivers, J.J. Smith of Appleton said he had no regrets.

"I have never hated crawling behind the wheel once," he said. "I just love racing."

J.J. Smith

His name is Jerry James Smith. It was shortened to J.J. Smith when he went to race in USAC. It was the same year that Jerry "Medina" Smith went to USAC and there already was a Jerry Smith racing on the circuit when they got there. With three Smith's on the circuit he agreed to be called J.J.

He started his career at the age of 15 just "fooling around" with a couple of friends. They had a 1936 Chevrolet that they asked him to drive at the asphalt quarter-mile Outagamie track. His parents, farmers in the Appleton area, hated racing so he knew it would do no good to ask them to sign the waiver permitting him to race at that young age. So he forged a signature on the waiver and lied his way in. Eventually he told his parents what he was doing.

At Outagamie they lined drivers up for the race in the order they came out of the pits. Smith came out last that first night and he ended up dead last in his first race. For one reason or another he always seemed to be the last one out of the pits and it wasn't until the end of the season that he won a race. As usual he came out of the pits last and was all set to start at the back of the pack when the flagman took things into his own hands. He turned the field around and Smith now had the pole position. He won his first race going around the track the opposite way.

In 1958, his second season of racing, he and a friend bought a Plymouth coupe. In 34 years of racing it was the only race car he has ever owned. "I like to hire myself out," Smith says. "I never had enough money to buy what I felt would be a good car. Besides, I've always felt that if you own the car, you drive it more carefully in an attempt to preserve it. If you don't own it, I think you do better. I've always been lucky. There has never been a year that I haven't had a ride."

"It is a different way of racing," says his wife Nancy. "Every time there is a new owner, you acquire a new set of friends and crew members. It is like being part of a whole new family."

In 1958, Smith began to qualify for the first and second heats and he won some semi-features at Shiocton and Outagamie. He drove the Plymouth for a couple of years and then sold it and began to drive a 1934 Chevrolet coupe owned by Charlie Spoehr that was capable of winning features at Leo's, Shiocton and Outagamie.

"I had a hard time winning my first feature, because veteran drivers at the time made it tough on those coming up. Finally, one night in a trophy dash, I boogered my way from the back to the front. They were ready to kill me when the race was over, but they respected me from that moment on." Smith drove for Spoehr for several years and then Spoehr dropped out of racing.

Then Lyle Schultz approached him with the idea of building a 1955 Chevrolet. Because it was the first to appear in the area, it contained a lot of experimental parts and was subject to many different set-ups in its initial year. As a result, it was not a winner that year. However, it was a winner the second year. Then Schultz and Smith parted ways.

Al Piette and Gene Wheeler asked Smith to drive a 1957 Chevrolet for them. He did and it was a persistent winner. Then they bought a 1955 Chevrolet from Wisconsin Rapids' Augie Winkleman. "I still remember going over to look at the car. I couldn't believe its 16-inch tires," Smith says. "I had never driven anything like it."

"Try it," said Winkleman, "You'll like it."

"I hot-lapped it hard," says Smith. "We bought the car and the hauler. It was my favorite car for a long time."

Then he switched to the Mustang with Mighty Mouse on its roof, owned by Terry Besaw. "We didn't do too well with that car," says Smith, "but then we built a 1969 Torino that was a winner."

In 1970, Shawano was still a stronghold for coupes, but the promoters were looking for a way to build the crowd so they invited J.J. Smith and Jerry "Medina" Smith, who was driving a 1967 Plymouth, to come up and make some noise and throw some dirt around. The headlines read, "The Late Models Are Coming." The crowd went from 1,300 to 3,100.

"We got pounded by the regulars who didn't want us there," Smith recalls. But before the year ended he had won seven features and track championship. The next year he was still the man to beat as he won six features there and repeated as track champion.

Smith won 40 features that season as he followed a circuit of Leo's, Shawano, DePere and Seymour. It was a high point for Smith and the dirt tracks. Crowds packed Shawano. At DePere, crowds of 5,000 arrived before seven o'clock and made it impossible to move about in the aisles. Fans who liked Smith chanted, "J.J ...J.J ...J.J." Those who didn't like him threw beer cans and shouted, "Go home."

"My main competitor during those years was 'Medina' Smith," says J.J. Smith. "When he began to fade

51

it was Roger Regath." J.J. won titles at Shawano in 1978 and 1979. He is still the track's all-time feature winner with a total of 44 victories. "Interest in dirt track racing began to fade in 1979 due to high costs," says Smith.

In 1980, he switched to asphalt and began to drive the B&B Racing Rander Car Camaro owned by Bruce Mueller. He drove for him until 1984, drove for Jim Seidl in 1985 and then took over a car owned by Gene Wheeler. "I had always driven a Rander Car, but Gene has a theory that you can't beat people racing the same thing they are. So he purchased a Left Hander chassis. It took us half of 1986 to get a feel for the car, but we're getting there," concluded Smith.

Driving late models on the asphalt was a challenge for Smith. "For the drivers like myself it is two nights a week plus the specials. It is hard to race against guys like Trickle who live in their cars. Trickle has always said I should go back to the dirt because there are only two guys who really know how to race on it — myself and A.J. Foyt. But I like the asphalt. The racing is tight and there are more drivers to compete against. Racing on the dirt changed. Ever notice that all of the dirt cars have advertisements for oil wells on their sides? It got expensive."

While most of his years were spent on the short tracks, he did race on the USAC circuit for three years beginning in 1966. Al Piette bought a 1965 Plymouth from Norm Nelson and asked Smith to be his driver. Roger Regath drove a Ford team car. Smith's best finish in those three years was a sixth at Raceway Park, Indianapolis.

Ask J.J. Smith what his favorite memories are and he puts at the top of his list his first 250-mile USAC race in Milwaukee. "The pit stops ... everything went right all day."

Second on his list is a 100-lap special in a Bruce Mueller car in 1981 or 1982 at Kaukauna. "I broke out early and led until the 50-lap mark. Then Ted Musgrave passed me, but I got the lead back and held it until lap

90. Then the front sway bar broke and I finished second to Trickle."

A third good memory was the 1986 ARTGO-NASCAR race at Kaukauna in which he finished fourth. "We really didn't have a plan but Trickle had told us we could make it on a tank of gas. Our mandatory pit stop was a touch-and-go one right before a long yellow. We finished the race with a half a glass of gas left in the tank."

For his wife, Nancy, the best memory goes back into the 1970's and a race at Seymour that paid 1,000 silver dollars. Smith had just sold a car to Herb Iverson and took a new one to the track that evening. When he blew a motor in it hot lapping, he asked Iverson if he could drive his old one because he knew he could win the race. Iverson agreed to let him do it if he could keep a percentage of the purse. Smith won and they put the bag of 1,000 silver dollars right on the hood of his car. It was his first big pay off.

Still another memory that Smith has comes from his days of driving the 1957 Chevrolet for Gene Wheeler. It was a 100-lap race at Shawano and Smith had taken an early and commanding lead. On the white flag lap, the right front spindle broke. Smith backed off the gas in an effort to nurse the car across the finish line. As he did so, Wally Jors thought he had blown an engine and, being a good Samaritan, tried pushing Smith. Smith did win.

Smith's worst wreck occurred one evening at Shawano. He had brought back the idea of throwing a car sideways on the dirt from the USAC trail. It was time trials and Smith let the car drift through under the flag-man, not worrying about having to make the corner. Another driver, coming out to time, said the sun was shining on his dash and blinding him. As a result, he hit Smith in the driver's door.

Once at Outagamie, Smith crashed and the six-cylinder engine came through the fire wall. The manifold, being on the driver's side, burned his leg. "Those early coupes had such heavy sheet metal that you could roll

53

them over and hardly dent them," Smith says. "We went to shoulder straps because drivers would flip and the narrow seat belt would cut into their hips. They were Army surplus tank shoulder straps."

And there have always been the good times after the races. Right down the road from Kaukauna used to be the Pit Stop Tavern, a place where many of the drivers and crews stopped after the races. "There was a guy from Wausau that used to come in there and he would always lay a $100 bill on the bar and say we were going to party until it was gone. The guy had been in a motorcycle crash in which he claimed to have broken 127 bones and lost all his teeth. As the evening would wear on, he would stage a fight with someone right next to some good looking girl sitting on a bar stool. As this supposed fight was about to break out, he would take out his false teeth and hand them to the unsuspecting young lady and ask her to hold them. The look on her face was worth a million dollars as she began to realize what she had in her hand."

'AN ACT YOU WON'T BELIEVE'

Canadian Jack
defies death

Don't leave after the feature, Don Ruder told the crowd at Golden Sands Speedway. "We have got an act that you won't believe. Canadian Jack racing through fire and flying through the air!" Then Ruder turned off the mike and said to Minnow Mall, the flagman who had joined him in the announcing booth in the infield, "Where does Sam Bartus find these guys anyway?"

Canadian Jack looked like leftovers from a junkyard dog's picnic. Two brown teeth smiled through a face with no fat, in need of one hundred bars of Lava soap. An extra notch had been punched in the cracked belt to hold up his faded Levis. Beneath the one sleeve of a grease-filled T-shirt was a blue line tattoo of a snake entwined around a dagger. The other arm pleaded, "Mother." When he spoke, each word echoed as if it were traveling through a great hollow tunnel before it arrived on his lips. Canadian Jack didn't defy death. He was death!

"There he is now," Ruder continued the hype, "preparing his motorcycle for a ride through a wall of flames. If that cycle falters at the wrong time, Canadian Jack will be fried alive!" Then Ruder turned off the mike. "I wouldn't let the guy tune my lawn mower."

Canadian Jack rode his motorcycle around to the back stretch as a test, popped a wheelie for the sake of the crowd, then streaked back to ignite the barricade. It may have looked impressive from the stands, but close up the barricade was nothing more than two two-by-fours with some laths holding them apart. When Canadian Jack rode between the two-by-fours, his head barely touched the bottom lath.

"Did you see that?" Ruder screamed. "Canadian Jack has just defied death! Give the man a round of applause." Then Ruder said to Minnow, "I could do that on my Lawn Boy in low gear."

It took Canadian Jack forever to set up the next stunt. He said the slant of the front straight was giving him difficulty. Ruder relayed the message to the crowd, begged their patience and put in a pitch for another beer.

Finally, everything was set. Canadian Jack was going to fly over a ramp and T-bone another car. To spice it up, an explosive had been set under the ramp. If Canadian Jack did not make it over the ramp before the explosive went off, he chanced being blown to bits.

The explosive was in place. Canadian Jack jumped in an old junker, circled the track for what seemed an eternity, then stopped to light the long fuse. He jumped back in the auto and circled the track. Then it happened, just as he was approaching the ramp. There was a weak explosion. It was not the kind that would destroy man and machine, but it was enough to topple the ramp. Canadian Jack's car became entangled in the planks.

"Is Canadian Jack still alive?" Ruder asked the crowd. Then he looked at Minnow and shook his head slowly. "Why couldn't we put the money into a second feature?"

Next, Canadian Jack was going to drive a car, the trunk open and filled with blazing hay bales, around the track. "Can Canadian Jack do it? Can he make it back to the starting line and leap out before the gas tank in that automobile explodes?" Ruder was at his best. Then he switched off the mike and said to Minnow, "Look at the size of that flame. You couldn't roast a marshmallow over it. I'll spit on it and put it out when he gets back here." Ruder never had the opportunity. The motor in the car quit on the back straight. The crowd started heading for the exit before Canadian Jack's grand finale.

It took forever to set up the ramp again. Canadian Jack was going to fly an amazing distance through the air and then let four cars cushion his fall. "This will take speed and courage," Ruder told the remaining crowd. "If he falls short, he could kill himself." Canadian Jack circled the track. As he approached the ramp, he took his hands off the steering wheel and reached for the arm rest on the passenger side as a means of protection. As he did, his foot slipped off the accelerator. The car slowed on the ramp and barely made the top edge. It teetered for a moment and then dropped to the track directly beneath the ramp.

Ruder just looked at Minnow. Then he whispered, "This is one thrill seeker that will die a natural death."

JOHNNY McNAMARA

McNamara becomes hero of the day

Johnny McNamara of Baraboo began driving in 1953. An old friend, Dick Davis, had a shop and raced. Johnny used to frequent the shop and, even though he didn't have a driver's license, he decided at age 15 that he wanted to be a race driver. Since

Johnny McNamara

the promoters at the Portage and Baraboo tracks knew he was under age and would not let him race, Johnny traveled to Adams-Friendship and Verona and lied about his age. No one caught on and he was permitted to race.

Johnny's first race was at Adams-Friendship in a 1932 Ford Coupe that had been rescued from a salvage yard. He remembers starting on the front row in the feature, but he doesn't know where he finished except it wasn't last. He drove that car for two years at Adams-Friendship, Verona, Portage, Baraboo and Rio.

He ran the coupes for ten years and had at least a dozen of them. As far as he remembers there were three 1932 Fords, one 1933 Ford, three or four 1935 Fords, and a couple of 1940 Fords.

The most powerful one that he had was the last one

which was enlarged from 120 to 309 cubic inches. "It took five or six blocks before we finally found one that made it," Johnny says with a smile. "We had a special crank, special heads, GMC/Chevrolet truck valves, and a lot of other goodies in it. It was as strong as the 1957 Chevrolets we were racing against. It held together for over a year."

Some of McNamara's early competitors included Joe Jones, Lee Weber, Dick Durst, Moose Johnson, Miles Milius, Fuzzy Fassbender, Cal Breezer, and Rudy Bandt.

The early tracks that he ran on are gone now, but some of his best races and memories stem from those days. He never counted but he figures in his years of racing he has won a couple of hundred semi-features and about 30 features.

Baraboo was his home track. It started as a half mile but later, at the request of the city fathers, was cut to a third mile in an effort to reduce speeds. The track was located on the fairgrounds and drivers were going off the track and into the barns on the grounds. Johnny won a lot of races there before it closed in the late 1950's.

One incident stuck in his mind. He flipped his 1932 Ford coupe on its side and another driver came along and blasted him right in the roof. He was dazed, but he got out of the car. When he looked down the track he could see a pack of cars coming and he took off on a dead run. Not thinking clearly about where he was, he ran right off a 15-foot embankment. "I thought I would never hit the ground," he said.

On another evening Johnny, who was winning steadily, got pushed off the track by a gang of drivers. They thought he was gone, but he drove down into a field, got turned around, and came back on the track at the back of the pack. He drove through them all and won the race. The yellow never came out while all this was happening.

Portage Fairgrounds was another track that started out as a half mile and after two nights of racing was cut back to a three-eighths mile track. It was good and fast and Johnny loved racing there. Driving for Merl Newton of Bear Valley, McNamara at one point in his career won six straight semi-features there. At the same time that he was winning the six straight semi-features, Cal Breezer, who was also driving for Newton, won six straight features. There were no point championships in those days. Whoever won was the hero for that day. The next day had its own hero.

In those days, racing was rough and when you won consistently it got even rougher. The drivers at Portage told Johnny that they were out to get him and when they did he went through the back straight fence and into a drainage ditch. McNamara received a broken nose in the accident. It may have been one of his worst injuries because he has never had to be transported to the hospital in all of his years of racing.

The baseball field at Portage was in the center of the track and the dugouts were concrete and under the front of the stands. They stuck out from the stands and one night Johnny, coming down the front straight wide open, hit the concrete edge of the dugout. When Johnny came to, the motor was missing from the car and the car was on fire.

The most dramatic of all accidents occurred one evening when Johnny put the lights out in half of the city of Portage. "I got out of control and hit a light pole with the side of my car," Johnny recalled. "Then the car spun around and kissed the pole with its front end. The transformer that was hanging on the pole came right down and stuck in the hood of my car. There were big wires flying and sparks everywhere. I stood up on the door and jumped and ran. It knocked out the lights on that side of town."

Johnny once won a race at Portage on three wheels. "The left front wheel got knocked off right at the start of the race in a crash. The car dragged a little but it stayed on the track for about 20 laps and I won the race."

Johnny McNamara (37) takes the low side against Rocky Breezer.

At Adams-Friendship, McNamara also found time to liven up the action. One evening he got in a tangle with a bunch of cars coming out of turn four. He slid, out of control, right toward the flagman, who ran for his life when the car hit the sand bank in front of the judge's stand. The car got high enough to take the top of the stand off and then crashed into a wrecker parked behind the stand. In his years of racing there McNamara has vivid memories of cart-wheeling off the back straight.

One evening, however, Johnny was not the victim of an accident. His friend Dick Davis was and Johnny saved his life. "Davis was driving a 1955 Chevrolet for Newton. He crashed into a light pole and the steering column came back and hit him in the face. When I ran over to the car a safety person tried to stop me because there were loose wires and sparks everywhere. I slugged the person and kept on going. When I got there, he was hanging upside down in the car and there was blood everywhere. Dick was bleeding just terrible. I crawled in the car and got him out. Fortunately, the hospital was nearby. The doctors said he wouldn't have lived a half hour without medical attention. Dick lost an eye but he lived. I know in my mind he never would have made it if something hadn't been done immediately."

During those days of racing at Adams-Friendship, Johnny used his dad's old Dodge as a tow car. One evening the clutch went out on the Dodge on the way to the track. Johnny had to find a way to get his equipment back to Baraboo. He ended up pushing the Dodge with his race car. No one ever said anything, but he must have woke up half the people in Wisconsin Dells as they went through at four in the morning.

According to Johnny, Verona was a fun track to run, although if it rained you needed a wrecker to pull you out of the pits. The track was about 50 feet below the spectator area and was a great one at which to watch a race.

Sometimes getting to Verona was a project. McNamara had lost his driver's license, but was still driving his tow car when a police officer stopped him. The officer looked at Johnny and said, "I don't know you and you don't know me. Get going to the races."

Rio was a sandy, dusty track and it was hard to see over the hood of a car. "It was miserable," said Johnny. "I didn't race there very often." The worst dirt track according to Johnny, was Spring Green. It was a real dust bowl out in the sand by Arena.

Johnny claimed that the funniest thing that ever happened to him was at Griffith Park in Wisconsin Rapids. "I was racing a coupe and the rear spring broke. The drive shaft went right under the seat, which was made out of a 30 gallon oil drum. There wasn't any cushion and when the drive shaft started rubbing under the seat it got red hot. I was leading the race and I wasn't about to quit. I unhooked the safety belts and stood up on the straights and burned in the corners. I won! I ran that car for two years more and every time I looked at the seat a three-inch blue mark was right in the middle of the seat to remind me of that race."

Racing in the early days of his career also meant a lot of county fair races — Marshfield, Wausau, Lancaster, Darlington and Richland Center. At Darlington it was 30 feet from the back straight to the Pecatonica River. "I ended up in it," said Johnny. He also remembered going off the track at Wausau. "I was going down the back straight with my foot in it," said McNamara, "and when everyone else turned, I didn't. I couldn't see the curve. I went right through a concrete wall, a plank fence and ended up in a cattle barn."

In 1961, Johnny made the switch from the coupes to a 1957 Chevrolet owned by Merl Newton. He drove Newton's car for five years at such tracks as North LaCrosse, Wisconsin Dells, Oregon, Columbus, Griffith Park, Tomah-Sparta and Black River Falls. His was always among the top cars and he won track championships at Columbus and Oregon.

In the five years he only had one serious crash and that was at Wisconsin Dells when eight cars wrecked on the front straight. "Marlin Walbeck hit me in the driver's door. There weren't any door bars in the cars at that time and the impact knocked my seat loose. I had to get six stitches in my back. We had to straighten the frame of the car and do some body work."

In 1966, he drove his own 1965 Ford and then he drove a Mercury Comet for Dave Deppe of Baraboo. He also went to work for Deppe in his shop maintaining trucks.

In 1972, he drove for Deppe on the USAC circuit. The car was the same one that Deppe would eventually buy back and turn into the Buick that Dave Watson drove so successfully at Milwaukee. Then McNamara drove a Nova, followed by Camaros.

Johnny retired from auto racing to become involved in truck-pulling contests for a number of years. He was killed in an auto accident on Interstate 90-94 near his home in Baraboo.

1970
The bounty hunters

A south wind, still without the warmth of a summer sun and filled with snow, kept the crowd chilled as Tom Reffner used the race car of a former year, a 1967 Mercury, to win the first feature at Capital Speedway. By April 25, Reffner still hadn't finished his new racer, but he had finished ahead of the competition for the third straight week. Owner Sam Bartus offered a $100 bounty to anyone who could best him, but the beat went on. Reffner wins four straight. Bartus raises the bounty to $150. Reffner wins five straight. Bartus raises the bounty $175. Reffner finishes third in a 50-lap Memorial Day special won by Joe Jones. The race is a special one and doesn't count. Finally, on June 6, Johnny Ziegler collected the $175. Ed Hume finished second in his 1970 "Boss 429" Mustang. It would be a month before Reffner found his way back to winner's circle.

During the interim, Trickle used handling ability to edge out Hume and Ziegler. Then Ziegler came on to win two more, one of them a 50-lap Fourth of July Special. After the Fourth of July, the month was Reffner's, who was still driving his 1967 Mercury. On July 14, he won and then blew the engine on the way to the pits. He closed out the month with two more victories.

August looked like it would follow the same pattern, as Tom Reffner took the lead in the first race of the month. That lead dissolved when Ed Hume, on the way to a victory of his own, collided first with Back and then with Reffner. The month continued to be one of frustration for Reffner, as Ziegler won and then Bill Retallick took the checkered twice. Rich Somers took the final race of the year.

At Wisconsin Dells, the track remained a short quarter-mile but the season was one long on cars and purses. Sixty cars showed for the opener, and it was announced that there should be one hundred cars out when everyone had theirs built. Marv Marzofka tied Marlin Walbeck for fast time and then went on to win the feature.

Chilly winds couldn't keep a near-capacity crowd from returning the second evening to see Marzofka win again. In the semi, it was Ed Nichols of Portage, followed by Buck Linhart of Union Center and Norm Bartnick of Portage. On June 6, there were 87 cars present, but it was once again Marzofka who grabbed the biggest share of a $3,000, 50-lap special purse.

Jim Sauter won, and then a quartet of new faces filled the local headlines: Roy Schmidke, Chuck Hosig, Ev Fox and Dick Trickle. Tom Jensen won, then Marzofka, and then Dick Trickle closed out the first half of the season by winning a 100-lap feature. Trickle won the event on a flat rear tire. Early leader Dave Field wasn't as lucky. After leading until lap 49, he departed with a flat right front tire. Trickle then outmaneuvered Sauter in traffic and bumped Joe Shear repeatedly as he made his way to victory lane.

Marzofka dominated the features at Wisconsin Dells in the month of July with two firsts and two seconds. He was shaded once by Sauter and once by Reffner. On one occasion, in which he eventually won, he collided with Marlin Walbeck, and it took pit crews fifteen minutes to get the cars untangled. Dale Walworth was busy sweeping up semi victories over Buck Linhart, Dick Ambrose and Bob Jusola. Gary Muchow destroyed his car, and Art Link puffed deeply on his cigar after winning a consolation race.

On August 8, after setting fast time eight times in nine weeks, Marv Marzofka broke the track record with a

65

Dells Motor Speedway

LaCrosse Interstate Speedway

12.96. Forty-eight late models and 40 hobby cars showed up, as Trickle won the feature in his 1969 Torino. Jimmy Back was raging through the land like a roaring lion, and he took the next feature event. Roy Schmidke and Billy Wirtz then surprised everyone with wins. In the final feature to be run in the summer of 1970, Jimmy Back edged out Marlin Walbeck by a fender length. The season championships, scheduled for September 12, were rained out. But it was one of those seasons that had contained so many cars and so much excitement that people came and sat in a steady downpour staring at the cancellation sign in disbelief.

Sam Bartus and the CWRA made up their differences during the off season, and in the season opener at Golden Sands, Tom Reffner held off Marv Marzofka and

Marlin Walbeck to win the feature.

The second event of the year was a demolition derby. Jim Back drove through a five-car crash to win the feature. On lap 22, Dick Trickle had the lead but was being passed by Tom Reffner. The two touched going into turn two, and Trickle's car shot into orbit off the 12-foot embankment. The car then spun in midair and slammed into the retaining wall backwards. Following too close to avoid the action were Marzofka, Walbeck and Larry Sparks. However, Trickle's car wasn't the only one to try flying. In a race previous to the feature, Ed Nichols brought the fans to their feet and the kids to the fence when he hit Bob Agena as the two came out of turn four and made a final dash to the finish line. Nichols' car flew across the finish line in midair and then destroyed itself in a crash landing that involved a number of flips.

If Tom Reffner found his face on bounty posters at Capital Speedway, the whole CWRA race crew would be hunted at Golden Sands. Early in the season, Sam Bartus decided that they were the toughest guns in the Midwest and offered a $150 bounty to any person who was not a member of the CWRA who could win a feature. On May 15, Jim Sauter, at the time an outsider, collected. His victory was also the advance warning of something that would be much more momentous. It signaled an end to the stranglehold that Fords had on the tracks in central Wisconsin. Sauter was driving a 1967 Chevelle.

The next evening of racing, it was Jimmy Back who won the feature, but it was Jim Sauter who erased his qualifying record that night with a 13.36. Albert Getzloff won a pack-style spectator race that evening in his own inevitable way. Positions were assigned by arrival time, and to make sure he and a friend had the front positions, both arrived in mid-afternoon. When the green flag dropped, from his inside pole position, he stood on the gas and planted his right front fender solidly in Turzinski's door. Getzloff kept his foot mashed to the floor and, finally, as they entered the front straight, Turzinski lost control and flipped his GTO over on a car that had gone off the track the instant the green had dropped.

Marzofka missed a sweep when Marlin Walbeck took the fast heat; then Trickle did get a sweep after having his hood and fenders removed in an accident. While Trickle took everyone's scalp in the racing part of the program, he almost lost his own in a demolition derby that followed. He was busy trading blows with Sam Bartus' Cadillac when flames broke out and traveled quickly on the gas from a ruptured gas tank under six cars, including Dick's. Trickle bailed out of his car, only to be stopped short and sent sprawling by a rope that was tied to his leg and the frame of the car as a substitute seat belt.

Ron Beyer celebrated the Fourth of July by destroying his car against the wall. Jim Sauter was about to celebrate a victory when his transmission broke and Marzofka swept him up. Sauter would return for a belated celebration the next week. A week later, Tom Reffner got a victory in between ambulance runs. The evening started out with Roger Gulmire sailing 55 feet through the air and into the wall. He was taken to the hospital to be treated for leg injuries. Then, in the feature, Larry Sparks was destined to take a trip under the flashing lights when he swerved to miss the fast qualifier of the evening, Tom Jensen, who was having troubles of his own. Ron Beyer crashed into Sparks, who was then given a double jolt when Marzofka tail-ended Beyer.

Marzofka won a feature. Larry Detjens' name appeared as a semi-feature winner. Then, Jimmy Back went on his mid-summer's rampage. Back blasted Reffner and Marzofka in a mid-season fifty-lap race and then came back to lower the qualifying record to 13.16 and win another feature. Old Timers were given a chance to do their thing, and Don Ruder won the race in Trickle's Torino. Jere O'Day and Don Lewis proved how serious they were about racing when, in the heat of battle, they crashed in turn two.

Modifieds versus late models became an attraction, and in the first meetings, the modifieds held a distinct advantage. Then Back, Trickle and Marzofka gathered $4,000 together and sent a man south for special gumbo qualifying tires. The tables were turned. Back lowered the qualifying record to 13.13 and then came back to win the feature, ahead of Trickle and Marzofka.

Tom Reffner took three straight, with Back on his bumper, and then Dick Trickle won the 100-lap finale, with Dave Fields on his bumper so close that he gave Trickle a few taps. That feature win gave Trickle his 21st of the year and broke a tie with Reffner.

Elsewhere on the circuit, Wausau opened with Phil Bickley as the promoter. Larry Wehrs built a new super speedway at West Salem, and Jim Sauter established himself as the track favorite.

The first Oktoberfest became a reality. Ron Waite, Bob Zynda, Floyd Fairfield, Merlin Weinfurter, Glen Zant and Tom Jensen dominated at Adams-Friendship. Marv Marzofka went to Minnesota and cooked behind the thin firewall in his car but scored the most impressive victory of his career by winning the IMCA Northland 300 at the Fairgrounds.

1971
Lightning
on the horizon

When the 1971 season opened, a new third-mile track greeted fans at Wisconsin Dells. The cycle had been completed. Except for Wausau, the circuit was now composed of larger tracks that could accommodate swifter speeds of the professional class of driver that was emerging from the ranks in central Wisconsin. As one looks over the list of winners in 1971, one name begins to take precedence over all others. It was the eve of a record-setting venture by Dick Trickle.

At Wausau, the Lady in Black of the central circuit, Trickle dominated the action, and by August 5, he had won seven features. On July 1, he set a track record of 14.27 and then lowered it to 14.09 the following week. His march to victory on the tricky quarter-mile was interrupted on occasion by Reffner, Marzofka, and Dick Schultz of Wausau. In the semi-feature, old pro Sonny Immerfall was challenged by such youngsters as Dick Joss, Jim Hornung, Dennis Paasch, Bob Mackesy and Warren Droesser.

Friday night scattered the action to Adams-Friendship, West Salem and Capital Speedway. The CWRA was absent for the first three programs at Capital Speedway, and Don Leach, Dave Watson and Joe Shear benefited. Then, Dick Trickle debuted a new Torino, set a track record of 19.74, and had a string of three victo-

**Bill Gronley of Reedsburg became the
flagman of the central circuit.**

ries halted by a crash. Bill Retallick held Trickle off in
the next program and collected a bounty for doing so.
Then, Trickle set another record, 19.43, passed Don
Leach on lap 20, and went on to an easy victory.

Rain, a broken rear axle and Johnny Ziegler were the
only things that interrupted Trickle's march to victory
for the rest of the season at Capital. Tom Reffner won a
50-lap feature in late June when Trickle fell from the
lead with mechanical problems. In mid-August, rain

helped Bob Jusola win. While Johnny Ziegler held Trickle at bay once, usually it was Trickle who either jumped off to a commanding lead or closed an insurmountable gap as on the evening that Jimmy Back received the Sports Father of the Year Award. Back could only watch in the mirror and then the windshield as the purple Torino swept him up.

Semi-feature winners at Capital Speedway came from far and wide and included such names as: Lyle Nabbefeldt, Whitey Gerken, Steve Manke, Bob Beattie, John McNamara, Ron Blum, Rich Bickle and Ron Scalissi.

While Trickle, Reffner and Back headed south to Capital on Friday nights, Marzofka and Jim Sauter headed west to dominate the action at West Salem Speedway. Sauter won the first three features before Marzofka narrowly beat him to the finish. The next week, Marzofka tore a wheel off his 1969 Torino in the fast dash and Sauter sailed to the finish unchallenged. Marzofka and Sauter traded victories, and then Rich Somers brought a halt to the two-man parade. Larry Behrens of Northfield, Minnesota, Don James of Bloomington, and Larry Detjens, who was driving a 1967 Dodge, made the Marzofka-Sauter affair an every-other-week thing. The specials at West Salem belonged to Tom Reffner and Trickle. Reffner won the Farm Progress Days' race and the 100-lap Old Style Cup. Dick Trickle had to replace an engine during warm-ups, but he still won the Oktoberfest race. Ed Nichols, Dale Walworth, Pete Mahlum, Bud Schroeder, Warren Droesser, Don Grant, Fred Beckler and Buck Linhart made their way through traffic and on to victory in the semi-features. In late May, Buck Linhart treated the crowd to the season's only rollover, as he did an end-for-end flip that destroyed his car.

The division of talent between Capital and West Salem brought a new list of winners at Adams-Friendship, which also ran on Friday nights. Floyd Fairfield, Clarence Greene, Del Kemnitz, Bill Wirtz and Ron Waite took the checkered flag for its victory lap. Dick Trickle made a surprise appearance on July 23 when rain forced the cancellation of the races at Capital Speedway. Trickle not only won the feature but set a track record of 15.79. He held the record at six tracks: Adams, Capital, Wausau, Wisconsin Dells and LaCrosse.

Saturday night brought everyone to Wisconsin Dells, where Howard Johnson and Jerry Benson unveiled a new third-mile oval. Don Miller of Portage broke his right hand and received rib injuries while testing the new walls. Jim Sauter won the inaugural in a new 1970 Chevelle. Marzofka was second in his 1969 Torino. The following week brought a capacity crowd to watch Jim Back's 1967 Ford roll in ahead of Somers and Marzofka. Bill Wirtz held off Trickle, and then Marzofka held off Wirtz.

Memorial Day weekend brought racing to Wisconsin Dells twice. On Saturday night, Reffner exchanged leads with Trickle five times before he won. It marked the third straight night that Reffner's 1969 Mercury Cyclone had edged his teammate's Torino. On Monday, Jim Back broke the track record by posting a 14.70, but Reffner remained hot and passed Trickle with four laps to go. Ed Nichols brought everything to a halt on lap 11 when he shortened his 1969 Torino against the retaining wall. Larry Sparks stood and watched during the semi as two wreckers pulled the remains of the new 1969 Chevelle away from the wall. Later in the week, Reffner continued to play from a hot hand, as he beat Trickle by the thickness of a bumper.

Traffic would be Reffner's "Achilles tendon." The next week he watched Trickle win from behind a pack of slower cars. However, when Trickle broke an axle the week after, it was Reffner who benefited more than any of the other 97 cars present. Marv Marzofka brought the crowd to its feet with a charge from last to second after wrecking and repairing his car. Trickle lapped the field in a special 100-lap event that closed out the month of June. He followed with another victory and then lowered the record to 14.52, but was denied a victory when

73

he spun into the wall during a bumper-to-bumper duel with Marzofka for the lead. Trickle beat Marzofka on the last lap the next time out. It was Trickle's 33rd victory for the year.

Then Marzofka and Sauter brought their West Salem show to the Dells, with the Ridge Runner coming out on top both times. Trickle came back to win, and then

Bill Retallick and Marlin Walbeck used slower traffic to finish first and second. On the last Saturday in August, Trickle lapped everyone but Retallick and Reffner, as he won his 50th feature.

Semi-feature drivers geared up for the new track also, and when the season was over, Dick Bentley, Lyle Nabbefeldt, Darrell Busch, Warren Droesser, Fred Bender, Norm Bartnick,

Crewman Albert Getzloff finds a moment to rest.

Greg DeLapp, Homer Spink, Dale Walworth and Del Kemnitz had shared victory circle.

The top drivers were absent from the opening race at Golden Sands, and Sonny Immerfall took advantage of it. Then, Dick Trickle won six straight. During the skein, he set the track record twice. On May 2, he lowered it to 13.10. Back said he would lower it into the twelves, but it was Trickle who showed the way with a 12.97. Each week, Sam Bartus added $50 to the bounty he was offering and when Reffner finally collected, it had reached $200.

Reffner won another event when he took the lead from Dave Field, and a pursuing Trickle broke a water pump. Jimmy Back battled fender-to-fender with Trickle the next time out. On lap 29, Back dipped to the inside, only to have Trickle cut down and send both spinning into the wall. Reffner inherited the lead and the victory. It was Reffner's turn to spin the next week, and he did it early, on lap two of a 50-lap Fourth of July Special. Trickle won.

Tom Reffner won again, and then Sam Bartus had everyone holding their breath and driving faster and deeper into the corners when he had the track repaved. When it was all over, five drivers had broken the track record 20 times, with Dick Trickle hitting a low 12.70. He then went on to win the feature. Marv Marzofka opened and closed August with victories. In between, it was Trickle, with Marzofka challenging, and Reffner, who won after he and Back touched, spinning Back out two laps from the finish. When the checkered fell over September's Wisconsin Late Model Championship, it was Back, Walbeck, Detjens and Jensen.

At Rockford, Retallick beat Trickle by half a car length. At Elko, Trickle won the Un-Cola and the Un-Cola Rematch. Reffner won the Old Style 200.

By the time the cars were parked in the garage for the winter, Dick Trickle had won 58 features. The storm stood poised on the horizon. Lightning was about to strike.

NABBEFELDT'S SIDEKICK
Roho the Rooster

Roho was the toughest rooster that ever graced a chicken house in Wisconsin Rapids. He had survived the perils of sleeping high in a tree, the thrown sticks, the pokes, the shaking branches. He had outrun the grim reaper, who would have placed his head between two rusty nails on a chopping block. He lived to race because he had participated in the law of Darwin to its fullest.

His racing career began when Lyle Nabbefeldt's daughter painted "The Chicken Coop" on the side of Lyle's 1934 Chevy. According to Lyle, "If you have a chicken coop, you need a chicken." Just as Roho settled on the chicken house roost with thoughts of being too tough to grace a frying pan, watched the current crop of yellow hatchlings and dreamed of a future harem, a long wire hook beckoned him to the land of speed.

"Chickens didn't have any rights," Roho, who was named after a famous fighting rooster in Mexico, was fond of saying in post-race interviews. "I remember once when Lyle was on a Wisconsin Rapids morning talk show, someone called in to say that he should be turned over to the Humane Society for making me ride in that car. Lyle evaded the issue by answering: 'Lady, you are worried about the chicken. What about me? I ride in the same car!'

"The pay was chicken feed. They didn't even wash the grease off me. In my first race, I was wearing a leash and got told to sit on the roll cage. In the middle of the first heat, I decided to wing-it out the window. What a

76

'fowl' up! There I was, dangling out the window between two cars, with Lyle trying to retrieve me and steer in traffic at the same time.

"Then there was the time some turkey hit Lyle in the rear, and we did three end-for-end rolls down the back straight at Golden Sands Speedway. Or at least Lyle and the car did. After Lyle crawled out, he started walking back to where it all began. First he found his cigarettes, then his lighter and finally me. From that time on, I didn't need a leash. I sat very quietly on the roll bar for fear of triggering that whole hen house of trouble again.

"The only time I ever got revenge was at Rockford. We were waiting in line for the start of the race, and I jumped out and did my thing right on the hood of Dick Trickle's No. 99.

"But I did get to party with the best of them. Every night after the races, I'd get placed on a bar, and the drivers would feed me peanuts and beer in a shot glass. The drivers still laugh about it. They say they could gauge how drunk I was by watching me. When sober, I'd take just a slight beakful. But as the night wore on, I'd slowly lean forward and bury my head in the beer right up to my eyes. Then I'd get sleepy and settle down on the bar.

"In the middle of the summer, Francis Kelly, owner of the Tepee Supper Club in Tomah, decided that I needed a week of rest and recuperation from the hard life of racing. Upon arriving at the supper club, they switched my refreshment to vodka, and it was down-right dangerous. Instead of hunching down on the bar after imbibing too much, I'd fall over backwards and land on the floor."

Roho's career lasted but one summer. He was partner to many a victory and many a crash. Often, he was the first to emerge from the billowing dust of a crash. The crowd in the old LaCrosse Speedbowl gave a rousing cheer as he was pulled from numerous wrecks. It would be nice to report that Roho died the death of a hero, but the autopsy read pneumonia.

1972
Color me purple and gone

"There is an appointed time for everything. A time to plant, and a time to harvest."

If Dick Trickle's consistent winning in 1971 was the seed of a record, then 1972 would produce the harvest. It started out with only a single bolt of lightning as a warning, an opening-day victory at Golden Sands. It built into a blinding rain. On May 13, Trickle scored his 12th win in 13 starts. On May 27, Trickle got his 15th win in 20 starts. When the last tremor was over, Trickle had a new record of 67 victories. He had become the winningest short-track driver in the United States.

Wednesday night on the circuit was North LaCrosse, and the season began in the old Speedbowl with Marv Marzofka trapping Trickle's 1970 Mustang behind some slower traffic and using that advantage to drive his new Moose Peterson Camaro to victory. Then next Wednesday, Trickle came back to beat Marzofka by a half lap. Tom Jensen came in third in a 1971 Torino. The next week it was Trickle again, as Don Grant came in second by holding off Marzofka and Reffner. Marzofka took two more and then it looked like Trickle had another in the bag before he tried using too much power, broke loose and permitted Marzofka to slip underneath. Back left Nabbefeldt and Reffner in the shadows, fighting for second. Trickle won again, and then the hard-chargers abandoned the speedway to John Brevick and Larry Anderson, who won the season finale which was held on August 10. In the class below, Tim Carlson spent the summer blowing the doors off the hobby stockers.

Wausau opened on the first Thursday night in May with Trickle beating Marzofka. It was the year of the pony car, and it was at Wausau that Larry Detjens debuted his 1972 Dodge Challenger before a hometown crowd. On June 22, Trickle struggled to get by Marzofka for four laps before finally doing so. Reffner, Detjens and Marlin Walbeck followed. It was Trickle's sixth victory in eight starts at the track. The beat went on.

Capital and LaCrosse Interstate both began the season on Friday night and again split the competition with Reffner and Trickle going to Capital and Sauter, Detjens, Marzofka, and Back going to LaCrosse. Rain won the first six events at Capital. When the clouds dispersed, Trickle took over. He was on his way to a fourth straight when his car came to a halt with a turned rod bearing and Joe Shear took over. It was the same evening that the throttle stuck on Johnny Ziegler's car going down the front straight. Fortunately for Ziegler, A.J. Moldenhauer was running on the outside and cushioned Ziegler's bullet-like ride into the wall in turn one. Not so fortunate was A.J. Moldenhauer, whose car was destroyed in the pinch. Fortunate were both drivers because neither was injured. "I was set up to pass Moldenhauer on the inside," Ziegler recalls, "when the throttle stuck. I went shooting toward the wall. Fortunately for me, Al was between me and the wall. I sliced him about in half. It was when he had the convertible, and I remember it was like hitting a big sponge. Of course, then everything flies and you can't see anything. After the dust and the dirt settled, I looked over at Al and had to laugh. There he was, sitting with his goggles going straight up and down on his face."

The next night out, Johnny Rank, who had crossed over from the Milwaukee modified circuit, looked like a sure winner until Trickle got out of traffic, closed the gap and passed him on lap 26. A loose coil wire was the gremlin that halted Trickle the next night out and Johnny Ziegler snared an easy victory.

Joe Shear brought out a new Camaro in mid-June, and with a bit of help from Larry Berwanger, it proved itself a winner the first night out. Shear broke into the lead on the fourth lap and was off and running before Trickle got out of traffic. But then Trickle put the pedal to the metal and made up half a track in six laps before being bumped out of contention by a spinning Berwanger.

Fate's dark finger pointed at Trickle a third time out. It looked like a runaway before Trickle's axle broke and Johnny Ziegler pounced on the opportunity to win. The next night, Reffner passed cars like they were parked, but then Trickle went on a rampage and won seven of the next nine races. A $6.000, 75-lap feature found him bringing a badly smoking Mustang home, just ahead of Joe Shear.

In mid-August, Johnny Rank lost control while on the power going down the back straight. The car slid along on the infield grass and then darted across the track and slammed into the fourth turn wall. Rank's seat belt broke and the rookie driver was hospitalized with a broken collar bone.

This was the year that Mike Miller drifted out of New Prague, Minnesota to test the waters of stiffer competition and made his debut at Capital Speedway in early September. In the semi-features, Tom Torbleau. Wally Kuehn, Cal Breezer, Vic Carr, Arnie Christen and Dick Morschhauser were the best of the lot.

LaCrosse Interstate also began its season on Friday night and once again it turned into a Sauter-Marzofka affair. Mert Williams of Minnesota won the opener with Detjens and Back glued to his bumper. Then Sauter tried every trick in the book for 11 laps to block off a charging Marzofka, but he finally drifted wide and Marvelous Marv went by on the inside. Sauter won. Marzofka won. Sauter won. Marzofka won. Then Sauter got caught in traffic, and Marzofka lost his brakes, giving Larry Detjens and Jimmy Back a chance to make the fans stomp and scream. Detjens motored by Back's Mustang. Then Back caught him on the back stretch and stayed beside him going through turns three and four. It was a matter of torque coming out of the turn, and Back sipped a victory beer when it was all over.

Marzofka won two more races, one of them a tin bender that got started when Pete Mahlum blew a transmission. Jon Chrest got crossed up with Lyle Nabbefeldt and Roy Schmidke, and they all came to a halt against the turn two wall. Then LaCrosse Interstate switched to Wednesday night, permitting those who had been racing at Capital to now be present. Trickle won three straight. In semi-feature action, John Brevick. Dale Walworth and Pete Mahlum got things started and then Larry Anderson became almost invincible.

At the Dells, Trickle won the opener on the last Saturday night in April and then dominated the month of May. June began with Larry Anderson spinning and

Trickle's first car had a rake wheel welded in it for a rollbar and a grader blade on the driver's side for his own protection. Since then, his cars became progressively faster.

Wisconsin Dells was dubbed "Home of the Biggies" because it attracted drivers like Ed Howe, who came to race against the local talent.

Trickle hitting him head on. Both cars lifted off the track and then dropped in a steaming, crumpled heap. Marzofka won. Johnny Rank finished second. Marzofka was a repeat victor the next night out. In a daring maneuver in the last 50 feet, Johnny Rank got by Sauter to finish second again.

Bob Jusola gave everyone standing behind the fence on the back straight something to think about. "Just as I was coming out of turn two, some guy came out of the infield and drilled me." Jusola's car took off and for a moment he was driving on the wall and the fence like a motorcycle rider in a wooden drum at a county fair. A member of the emergency crew, who didn't duck, later told Jusola, "I saw your exhaust pipes go by." Bob's car gained enough altitude to permit Marv Marzofka to drive underneath him before it crashed to the track.

Wisconsin Dells in July belonged to Trickle. He opened the month by getting the lead in two laps and beating Marzofka easily. It was his 32nd victory. Then he caught polesitter Johnny Rank and stormed off to victory. Finally, with an $8,230 purse for a 100-lap show, it was Trickle, Ziegler and Reffner, in that order. Marzofka did win the last race in July and Tom Reffner snatched up two victories to start out August. When the 100-lap special rolled around at the end of August, Trickle shoehorned a new 454-cubic inch engine in his Mustang and grabbed victory number 54.

Howard Johnson dubbed the Dells Motor Speedway as the Home of the Biggies. To prove that it was, he invited Michigan's Tom Maier and Ed Howe, "The Green Hornet," to the speedway for the first time and offered a $16,000 purse. Trickle won the 200-lap feature for victory 61. He was followed across the line by Marzofka, Howe, Maier and Shear.

Variety was the name of the game in the semi-feature, as Dale Walworth, Jim Sauter, Ron Waite. Gordie Platt, Tom Jensen, Larry Sparks, Bob Turzinski. Kato Thiesen, Dave Lalor and Larry Behrens all took home checkereds.

When the green went down on Sunday night at Golden Sands, Trickle was off and running. He set a track record of 13.09, turned back Marzofka three times and got a bounty slapped on his head. Then Lyle Nabbefeldt, who had escaped serious injury the Sunday before when the throttle stuck on his 1968 Camaro and crashed in turn one, won a 100-lap feature. He was saved a duel with Trickle when a coil wire came loose in Trickle's car. "Step Aside, The Snapper Has Arrived," was the motto on the hood of Nabbefeldt's car. Jimmy Back did everything he could to hold Lyle off the next time out, and it took 14 laps of rubbing doors before Lyle finally got by.

Trickle won two more and then blew an engine in the 50-lap mid-season championship, permitting Marzofka to beat Reffner. The championship race was followed by a 100-lap feature, and Trickle watched his tires fade as Larry Detjens roared to victory. Detjens outran Trickle again before Trickle posted another win. Reffner won with Trickle absent and then it was Trickle. In mid-August, Marzofka closed in on Trickle, bumped him, and although Trickle got back into the fray, he couldn't get around Marzofka.

Marlin Walbeck finished third. Trickle won a 100-lapper and closed out the track's program with a win. The beat went on.

On the larger circuit, Trickle nipped Rank after a 40-lap duel in Kaukauna's "Red" race. Trickle won the "White" race and then was beaten by Joe Shear in the "Blue" race. Reffner won Elko's Uncola 100. Trickle won the Northstar 300 by leading 242 laps. The Elko Old Style race was number 65 for Trickle. The MASCAR 300 at Odessa was number 66.

Then Trickle returned to Capital to track down Johnny Reimer's modified. They battled side by side on lap 28 and 29, and then Reimer drifted wide, permitting Trickle to pass. It was victory number 67. The season was over. If the sun set in a purple haze, it had reason to do so.

TOM REFFNER

Reffner debuts in an Oldsmobile

Tom Reffner's interest in auto racing began in 1958 when he accompanied his friend, Marv Marzofka, to Stratford Speedway. Marv's brother, Ron, had raced at Crown Speedway in Wisconsin Rapids and Marv decided that he wanted to follow in his footsteps. The car was a 1952 Studebaker that they had altered with an axe to look like a 1951 Studebaker, since the rules required that all cars be 1951 or older.

"Marvin was working at a Studebaker garage. He had a car which he had bought pretty reasonable, and he didn't have a title for it," Tom says. "I think we put a roll bar and a straight axle in it and that was about it. In those days, we didn't have any money to spend on engines or anything. If you wrecked an engine, you just went down to the junkyard and got another one. The sport was just kind of starting out and we lucked out and got in on the ground floor."

They arrived at the track with only one roll bar in the car and were not permitted to run because the rules called for a four-point roll cage. They went home and made the necessary changes and returned the next week. In his first night of racing, Marv won the semi-feature, which paid $40.

Reffner would continue to go with him for the rest of the summer. In 1959, at age 18, he raced his own 1949 Oldsmobile at Stratford and Wausau. At Stratford the fastest 40 cars, determined by time trials, raced. Reffner remembers the racing as dusty and bumpy. There was a lot of crashing and banging and the cars were dangerous. Still, strange as it might seem, when Griffith Park was the first track to be paved in the area in 1960 there was some apprehension about running on asphalt.

Leonard Trickle, Larry Carcy and Stan Johnson were some of his early helpers. Whenever Stan Johnson was connected with one of his race cars, it was apparent because Stan always insisted on painting a flying red horse on the side of the car.

Tom won his first heat race (the first heat) on Thursday night, August 4, 1960, at Griffith Park. On the same night, Dick Trickle won the fourth heat and a trio of Wisconsin Rapids drivers finished 1-2-3 in the feature — Jere O'Day, Don Ruder and Vic Kopacz. Reffner came back the next Sunday, August 7, and won another heat race. Ken Pankratz beat O'Day in the feature that evening. Of the 45 cars entered that night, 24 of them ran in the money. In one of his finest races that summer, he finished fourth in a feature at Griffith Park. Augie Winkleman won the race, followed by Herb Kurth and Dick Trickle. Besides Griffith Park, Reffner would continue to race at Stratford and Wausau.

The 1949 Oldsmobile remained a favorite of Tom's throughout his early career. One was retired when someone put sugar in the gas tank at Griffith Park. Tom went to the salvage yard to get another motor and, thinking they were the same, came home with a 1954 engine. However, they weren't the same and he had to switch to a newer body to use the engine. In a hurry to get to Black River Falls, he just tacked the roll cage in place. "It was that old optimistic viewpoint," he says now. "I won't get in a wreck." However, he did and he got knocked out and sent to the hospital when a crash sent the roll cage flying around in pieces in the car. He was back the next week.

While Gus Winkleman and Marlin Walbeck were dominating the feature races in 1961, Reffner was timing in and finishing well. Time trials at Adams-Friend-

Three of Tom Reffner's cars.

ship on one evening brought these results: Vic Kopacz, 19.52; Marlin Walbeck, 20.13; Tom Reffner, 20.16; Jere O'Day, 20.22; Dick Trickle, 20.25. On a different evening, Tom would finish third in the feature at Friendship. He would also finish third in a feature at Griffith Park on a night when 49 cars timed in.

In 1962 and 1963, Marlin Walbeck ran so strong that he found a bounty being offered to the driver that could beat him. At the same time, Tom Reffner was winning semi-features at Griffith Park and Wisconsin Dells.

In 1964, cars were divided into class by their body style. Reffner found himself racing in Class A. In June, the point standings were as follows: Class A: Walbeck, 566; Lyle Nabbefeldt, 401; Trickle, 391; Marzofka, 329; Fox, 324; Bredl, 219; Marcis, 158; Reffner, 144. Class B: Back, 181; Spink, 165; Hanson, 109; Link, 97; Bowden, 97. Reffner switched to Class B and by July 11 the standings would read Jim Back, 496, and Tom Reffner, 489. As the curtain came down on the season in September at Griffith Park it was Back, 911; John McNamara, 760; and Reffner, 654.

In 1965 Tom began to drive a 1954 Mercury for Jimmy Back in what was known as the "B" Main. Reffner won the B Championship race on May 23 at Griffith Park. He returned to victory circle at the Speedway on June 10th. Tom was second in the trophy dash at Black River Falls on June 12th. On June 16th, Reffner came in fourth in the second heat at Stratford. He returned to Stratford and won the semi-feature on June 20. By July 10, he was second in the Class B point standings at Griffith Park. Wayne Kittleson had 424 and Tom followed with 300. On July 10, Abel Marzofka Jr. beat him in the semi-feature at Tomahawk. The following night at Black River Falls he won the third heat race and finished fifth in the semi-feature.

As the 1965 season continued Reffner was consistently in the top five in the semi-features and he also began to set fast time for the Class B cars. The Central Wisconsin Speedways Association included Griffith

Park, Wisconsin Dells, Black River Falls, and Tomah-Sparta. On August 28, Marv Marzofka led the Class A standings with 2,635 points. Ev Fox was second, Trickle third and Lyle Nabbefeldt fourth. Tom Reffner had just moved into first place with 495 points. Wayne Kittleson was second with 449. Kittleson went on to win the Class B title.

A log kept by Tom during the early part of 1965 gives an insight into racing in the 1960's:

April 2: Car complete except for seat, drive shaft, and one door. 7:00-3:00

April 3: Painted car. Started pickup truck up but the oil filter was gone. 7:00-11:30.

April 4: Tried car out. Good on the low end but dead at higher rpm's. Jim's car seems to jump right and left too much. 1:00-6:00

April 5: Worked with Verlon on Olds. $10.00 torsion bars.

April 6: Back bought 1955 Ford one ton for $200. Worked with Verlon on the Olds.

April 19: Easter. Worked at Jim's. 6:00-12:00.

April 22: Played pool.

April 23: Worked on Jim's extended trailer tongue. 7:30-1:30.

May 1: Raced at Wisconsin Dells. I won the second of the three heat races and got third in the semi-feature. First heat = $35. Third semi = $30.

May 2: Raced at the Rapids. Got second in the second heat. Forced to run the feature and had third or fourth but #3 Chev bumped me and spun me out. Number 3 got third. I got 10th. Second = $15. Tenth = $10.

May 3: Changed tires on my car. Helped Back change transmission. He went from 1:62 to 1:48 with 4.27 rear end.

May 5: Went down to Griffith to try out 61 but Ruder wouldn't let us in.

May 9: Sunday. Went to Stratford in afternoon. Got second in the semi. $24. Night at Rapids. Third in heat $15.

89

Got smacked in the side on straight away by #33 Chev.

May 14: Went to Madison. Got rained out. Sam gave Jim $20. Let Jim keep it all.

May 16: Won trophy dash, was second in heat semi at Tomahawk. $75. Won fast time for semi, fourth in third heat + third in semi, $65, total. $25.00 for fast time.

May 19: Got fourth in heat. Tire went fiat in pits so we put one of Jim's new slicks on and moved into first place in the semi and the tire blew from rubbing on the spindle arm. $9.

May 20: Put new Merc spindle and lowered it 2".

May 23: Won trophy dash. Got bumped by #78 in heat. Axle broke in the semi. Was in second moving into first at Tomahawk. Got fourth in heat at Griffith. Hoffman held me back. Won semi. Heat = $10. Semi =$60.

May 30: Blew motor up. Put Dick's motor in.

Those were the last of Tom's personal notes for 1965. In 1966, he was moved into the feature or Class A division and he began the season by consistently running in the top five. On July 7 he won the feature at Wisconsin Dells, finishing ahead of Jere O'Day and Dave Marcis. On July 15 at Tomah-Sparta Tom jumped off to an early lead and held off Jere O'Day to take the feature. On August 18 at Wisconsin Dells Tom drove his 1963 Ford to a narrow victory over Dick Trickle's 1963 Ford and Marv Marzofka's 1961 Ford.

After the final race of the season at Griffith Park, awards were handed out. Marv Marzofka was the Class A champ (Trickle was the circuit leader); Gary Kneisley, Class B; and Roger Olson, Class C. Best Sportsman - John Brevick. Most improved driver - Dave Field. Hard luck driver - Everett Fox. Most cooperative - Homer Spink. Owner contributing the most to racing - Francis Kelly.

In 1966 Tom traveled outside of the state for the first time, competing in the first National Short Track Championships at Rockford.

In 1967 Reffner continued to drive for Jimmy Back. In May, Reffner won two features on the same day, one

Marv Marzofka and Mark Martin have plenty of advice for Tom Reffner.

at Wausau and the other at Golden Sands. Tom also won two features at the Dells in May. On July 13, he won at Griffith Park when the engine in Willie Wirtz's car blew. Two days later Dick Trickle moved from the back of the pack at the Dells to an impressive lead at the halfway mark. He was all alone on the last lap when a tire blew and he dropped out of the race. Reffner took the lead and won. The point standings at Griffith Park on July 18 read: Trickle, 900; Marzofka, 843; Reffner, 570; Back, 517.

The 1967 season continued with Reffner and Trickle dueling it out on August 6 at Golden Sands. Trickle repeatedly challenged Reffner during the race and finished with little more than a foot separating the cars. To add to the excitement, the left rear wheel on Reffner's car caught fire moments before he crossed the finish line.

In 1968, Tom bought a 1967 Ford from Jim Back and opened the season in a strong fashion at Golden Sands. He beat Marlin Walbeck on April 28 in the feature. On June 12 he worked his way through the pack at North LaCrosse Speedway and passed Ron Beyer on the outside for a victory. Early in the feature Lyle Nabbefeldt spun sideways on the front straight. About six cars avoided him but Dick Trickle didn't see him and slid into the soft shoulder beside him. They remained there as spectators for the rest of the race. Reffner won two features at Golden Sands in June and then won a $500 Firecracker 75 at the same speedway. In August, Reffner was second in points to Marlin Walbeck at Golden Sands. In the 100 lap State Championship Race held in September at Golden Sands the top three finishers were Walbeck, Back and Reffner.

On May 10, 1969, Jimmy Back broke the track record twice at Wisconsin Dells but Reffner would win the feature which paid $140. In June, Tom set a track record of 20:08 at Oregon. In July he won at Capital Speedway and then in his first appearance at Kaukauna, won a 50-lap race. Columbus put on a two-day program in late August and Reffner tied for first in the 200-lap feature and won a total of $1,126.

In 1970, Reffner drove his 1967 Mercury Comet to new heights. He won the first two features at Capital Speedway and had a clean sweep in the Golden Sands opener. On July 18 he scored his seventh win of the season at Capital Speedway. On July 23, 4,500 fans packed the North LaCrosse Speedway to watch Reffner win a 100-lap feature on the second night of racing there. He won at Sands and, after four wins in a row at Capital, had a bounty of $150 placed on him. By August 23 he had won 20 late model features. One of them was a victory over Al Schill, who was driving a modified, at Capital Speedway. As the season came to a close he was already preparing for the next by building a 1969 Mercury Cyclone fastback and a 1968 Mustang fastback for the tracks that would permit pony cars. He had also converted an old school bus into a hauler. The ultimate test came when he took his wife and crew plus Jim Back's mother, wife, and nine kids to Capital Speedway.

In 1971, Dick Trickle would begin his march to short track fame with 58 victories, but Tom would continue to do well and prepare for his own day of glory a few years later. In June, Reffner won a 50-lap feature at the Dells. At West Salem he won two of the biggest races of the year, the Farm Progress Days Race and the 100-lap Old Style Cup Race.

On the Saturday night of Memorial Day weekend, Reffner exchanged the lead five times with Trickle before winning at the Dells. It marked the third straight night that Reffner's Cyclone had beaten Trickle's Torino. On Monday, Back broke the track record with a 14.70, but Reffner remained hot and passed Trickle with four laps to go in the feature. Later in the week, Reffner beat Trickle again, this time by the thickness of a bumper. Two weeks later, with a field of 97 cars gathered at the Dells, it was Reffner again.

When Trickle set a track record of 12.97 at Golden Sands and won six straight races, promoter Sam Bartus offered a bounty. Reffner collected a total of $200 for finally beating Trickle. Reffner won three more features at Golden Sands in 1971.

In 1972 Dick Trickle won 67 races. Tom Reffner would remember 1972 because he suffered his worst crash at I-70 when a ball joint broke, triggering a wreck that would leave him with broken ribs. The only wreck that has come close to matching this one was a wreck at Elko, Minnesota, in which he was knocked unconscious. The interesting fact about this wreck was that when Tom regained consciousness in the hospital he had this deep feeling that his race car was too safe to be injured in and that the wreck must have occurred while driving his hauler home from the race. When the doctors wouldn't let him see his sons he became even more convinced that such was the case. Obviously, they were dead. It was only when he saw them that he was convinced that he was there as a result of a racing accident. Reffner won about a dozen features in 1972, but often had to settle for second behind Trickle.

In 1973 Jimmy Back, with Robert Holmes as his sponsor, won 17 features. The pair returned in 1974 to win

Suddenly, the race is over and the heat of the day catches up with Tom Reffner.

19 features. Reffner held on in 1972 and, amid wind and snow showers, opened the season at Capital Speedway with a victory in his Bredl Auto Mustang. In June he won both of the features in the Marc Times Invitational at Capital Speedway. Reffner won at Golden Sands on June 24 and then on Wednesday night at West Salem, when Trickle blew a motor in a heat race, slid in the oil and tore the right front wheel off his car when he hit the wall. Reffner would battle again with Trickle at Wausau on July 5th and win.

In April 1974, Reffner narrowly beat Trickle on April 28 at Golden Sands. He won one of the Tri-R promotions features at Wausau and the "Blue" race at Kaukauna. Tom finished first and second in two 104-lap events to take Kaukauna's North American Championship and then borrowed an engine to win the track's Rawhide 100. His worst accident of the year occurred at Slinger when another racer bounced off a cement wall, flipped on top of Reffner's car and caved in the roof. At the time, Tom was preparing a 1974 AMC Javelin for competition.

The year of 1975 was to be Tom Reffner's finest hour.

With an Ed Howe Javelin and Pete Haferman as his mechanic he made a strong bid to surpass Trickle's short track record of 67 feature wins.

At LaCrosse he was stopped twice on his way to the title. On one occasion his engine went bad. On another occasion, Jim Pierson spun trying to pass Larry Detjens. Dick Trickle hit Pierson and bounced into Jimmy Back. Billy Oas and Tom Reffner both hit the cars ahead of them and were eliminated. He won the Dr. Pepper 150 and in the course of the season beat Detjens, Shear, Marzofka and Trickle.

A sign of Reffner's character occurred the next spring when the promoter at New Smyrna wrote and sent out hundreds of press releases saying that one of the entrants was Tom Reffner, whose 68 victories had eclipsed Trickle's 1972 record of 67. Tom called him and asked him to change the release. He had not won 68 features. The exact count was 67. Tom asked him to correct the release.

By the end of the 1976 season, Tom would win 39 features. It was not 67, but the year would include a memory of its own. Tom would win the World Cup 400 at Odessa, Missouri. His share of the winnings was $10,000, the largest purse of his career. If 1975 was his finest season this was his finest day.

After the race, Reffner said the key to winning was not pushing too hard at the beginning of the race. "It's a really tricky track. You don't want to go out and push hard at the beginning, because it will get you at the end." The $10,000? "We're going to spend it on motor parts," said Tom as he spoke of building a 1977 AMX Hornet for 1977.

Tom would run the AMX Hornet until 1980. In 1977 he had 19 feature wins. He ran very strong at Golden Sands where he had six feature wins. In 1978 Reffner had 21 feature wins and also won the ARTGO championship. Four of those victories came in a row at Elko, Kaukauna, Golden Sands, and West Salem. In 1979 Tom won 16 features.

95

Tom's statistics with AMC cars from 1975 to 1979 are outstanding. In 1975 he ran 115 features, won 67 of them, and set 16 new track records. In 1976 he ran 125 features, had 39 firsts, and set nine track records. In 1977, in the Bemco Hornet, he ran 107 features, won 19 of them, and had one new track record. In 1978, he ran 87 features, won 21 features, and had eight new track records in a Frings car. In 1979, he ran in 61 features, won 16 of them, and had three new track records.

It was in 1979 that Reffner had the wreck at Elko and that slowed his career for a period of time. He dropped from first in the ARTGO standings and then went on to win only four features in 1980 and seven in 1981. In 1982 he was back on the winning trail with eleven feature victories. From 1967 to 1982, Reffner won 278 features and set fast time 245 times.

From 1983 to 1987, Reffner was never below 13 in the feature win column and his high was in 1987 when he won 22 features. Some of his finest victories have been at Capital Speedway in the October Nationals. He won the title in 1983, 1984, and 1986. After being in the top three in CWRA points since the beginning of their points championship, Reffner won the title in 1987. He continued to prove that he was a top Midwest driver.

Since his early days when Leonard Trickle and Stan Johnson helped on the car, Reffner has had a lot of people in his pits. Jimmy Back has been a constant companion, along with John Bovee, Dick Skibba, "Sarge" Sether, Pete Haferman, Keith and Mike Minash, Charlie O'Keefe, Pat Hauser, Paul Smith and Ed Gille. And probably most important, his own family, his wife and sons Baird and Bryan. It takes a lot of people to make a great career possible, and Tom's has been all of that.

1973
Back is back

J immy Back was a legend the first day God thought of him. As a builder and master of the midnight thought, his cars were always fast. Add Robert Holmes as a sponsor and a Bemco chassis and Jumping Jimmy was ready to set the racing world on its ear in 1973 and 1974. In 1973, he won 17 features. In 1974, he raised the number to 19. Track records fell everywhere.

LaCrosse Interstate was where the week began and, although Billy Oas won the opener off the pole, Back came back strong with three straight victories. On each evening, Dick Trickle would be his chief adversary. The fourth night out, Back got into a tangle with Dan Przyborowski, and Marv Marzofka went on to win the 100-lapper. On that same evening, Johnny Rank would be hospitalized after hitting the wall on the first lap of the race.

Trickle beat Back the next time out. Then Joe Shear moved in and with a masterful piece of driving, he blocked off Trickle lap after lap to take a feature. Back came back to beat Marzofka. Bob Jusola, The Flying Finn, gave people from Minnesota reason to be proud, and then Dick Trickle won two more races. Once again, Johnny Rank found himself the victim of misfortune when he lost a wheel and crashed. A young talent would soon be forced to retire early as a result of the injuries incurred in two summers of racing. As the regular season closed, it would be Back who would flash across the finish line ahead of Trickle and Marzofka, taking

Back's family, real and adopted, has always been large and given him a great deal of support.

both the race and point title.

On Thursday night, the show moved to Wausau, and then on Friday night, everyone headed for Capital Speedway. It may have been spring and reflexes a touch slow, but Boyce Sparkman, Whitey Harris and Dick Trickle brought the crowd to the edge of its seat at Capital, as they went three-wide down the back straight. Trickle would be the eventual winner, with Harris coming in second and the fast timer of the evening, Marv Marzofka, finishing third.

According to Marv Marzofka: "Jimmy Back is probably the best philosopher in the world. The problem is nobody can remember what he said in the morning. The last thing you remember is Back standing there in a perilous lean, making half a stab at your belt buckle with his cigarette hand, while thoughts begin with a name and wander off into nowhere... 'Now Dick...' 'Now Tom ...'"

Ron Petrowski, a former member of Back's crew, once said: "It must be the sleep that makes me sick. I always feel pretty good when I go to bed." And there was the time that the author of this text arrived at Capital Super Speedway, only to be greeted with these words, "You should have been here last Friday night. There was your story! Jimmy Back and his crew partied until six in the morning, and then they only went home because Jimmy ran out of cigarettes." Later Ted Musgrave would plead, "Father, you have to bless these coolers so they don't give us the same headaches they did last week!"

On the second evening of racing at Capital, Marv Marzofka would be involved in a wreck that would sour his racing at Capital forever. As Marzofka was passing T.K. Shear coming down the final stretch, Shear lost control and sent Marzofka crashing into the wall in turn one. As Marzofka recalls the event, everything seemed to happen in slow motion. "I saw the windshield drift slowly away and break against the wall," Marzofka said. He was still dazed when he crawled out of the car.

He rebuilt the car in one evening and set fast time at the Dells the next evening but has always remained hesitant about racing at Capital since then. "When you race at Capital, you throw the fenders in the truck, then the doors, then the hood, and finally you load the rest of the car," is how he feels. It is similar to Jimmy Back's thoughts about racing at Rockford: "You take two cars. One you race, and the other you bring home."

Joe Shear embarrassed Trickle by taking the lead away from him and taking a victory on the third evening of racing at Capital. Trickle gained revenge by soundly beating Shear the next time out. Johnny Ziegler won the next feature but only after initiating another major crash. Ziegler spun on lap 16, and when Trickle spun to avoid hitting him, Trickle was hit by Dave Watson. The purple Mustang hit the wall with such an impact that it lifted from the track and burst into flames. When the car finally came to a rest in the infield, a dazed Trickle climbed out and fell to the ground. Later, he went home and began building a new car.

It was the beginning of the era of twin features, and Tom Reffner started it off with a double victory in the

MARC Times Invitational. The first time out, he beat Terry Bivins and Whitey Harris. In the second 75-lap event, he outran Dick Trickle and Bob Senneker.

Fred Bender still laughs about his first race at Capital, "When I finished, both front fenders were gone, and I didn't realize it. By the end of the season, you could walk out any corner of the car." By 1973, he was the most improved driver on the circuit, and to prove it, he began June by beating Joe Shear.

While Jimmy Back won two races and was always in contention, the rest of the season at Capital Speedway was a trade-off between Shear and Trickle. Shear won five races and dropped the track record to 19:140. Trickle also scored five victories, including the Pepsi 100 and the Badger Monza 150.

The semi-feature winners were varied and included many new names: Roy Shackelford, Willie Reints, Sam Reakes, Tom Greenlee, Conrad Morgan, Bob Wawak, Larry Leach, Wayne Swartwout, Dick Crawford, Arnie Christen, John Speer and Bill Retallick.

The season began at Wisconsin Dells with victories by Marzofka and Back and then tragedy struck. Jim Back set a track record of 14:543, and Dick Trickle won the feature, but fans left in a somber mood knowing that Lyle Nabbefeldt had lost his life during time trials in an accident in turn one.

The next Saturday night, Jimmy Back saw enough through his welding-specked glasses to steer through a ten-car wreck — that included Dave Field, Larry Detjens and Billy Wirtz — and take the checkered. Marlin Walbeck took third.

Marzofka beat Ziegler and Reffner, and then Terry Bivins won a 100-lap special. It was a race in which Dick Trickle had everybody sucking pond water until his engine blew on the 78th lap. Trickle would end up watching the next race from the infield also, after trying to slip between Marzofka and Shear, who were fighting for the lead. The daring move caused all three to spin, but Marzofka recovered in time to win. Trickle encountered still more difficulties when in late August he crashed into the wall after a tie rod broke during an attempt to pass Rich Somers. Marzofka, Back, Sauter, Detjens and Somers shared the honors in the remaining races.

The semi-feature at Wisconsin Dells was a mix of names: Paul Christianson, A.J. Moldenhauer, Ron Waite, Roy Schmidke, Dick Grave, Harold Bahr, Buck Linhart, Homer Spink and Mike Waddell.

Lyle Nabbefeldt, famous for his races with Roho the Rooster, was killed in time trials at Wisconsin Dells.

At Golden Sands, Marv Marzofka won the opener without too much trouble, but in the second race, Jim Back, Whitey Harris, Marzofka and Tom Reffner crossed the start-finish line like a pack of angry bees. Dick Trickle spun out trying to pass the whole group, and Jimmy Back was declared the winner.

Winners changed every week, with Dick Trickle taking the Fourth of July special, Rich Somers the mid-season championship and Jimmy Back the final race of the year. Bob Turzinski brought the final feature of July to a halt when the throttle stuck on the front straight. The car climbed a sand pile at the end of the straight and crashed head on into a concrete wall, knocking Turzinski unconscious.

Dick Trickle led the way in capturing out-of-state specials. In April, he won a 200-lap feature at Rolla, Missouri, and then moved to Odessa the next day and won a 50-lap bumping contest with Larry Phillips. In May, Trickle returned to Missouri, won a 150-lap race at Springfield, and then returned to Odessa to take two more features. Tom Reffner won the Illiana Championship, but Trickle returned to the victory lane at Rolla and Odessa. He also powered his 1970 Mustang to victory at the Minnesota Fair. Trickle won at Rockford early in September, but the final showdown at the speedway went to Mike Miller, who was still hauling out of New Prague, Minnesota.

1974:
Back stays hot

Wausau fans went home happy on opening night. Their hero, Larry Detjens, picked his way through traffic and then zeroed in on Dick Trickle. By lap 17, he had passed him, and the only thing left between Larry and the checkered flag was laps to be counted. Trickle reversed things the next night out and led Detjens and Jimmy Back to the finish. Detjens found himself in second place again on the third evening of racing when Marv Marzofka and his 1974 Camaro overpowered everyone.

Then Dave Field got through traffic early and left Marzofka and Back wishing there were more laps to be run. Marzofka came back to defeat Field the next evening of racing and won another after that. In both, the Lady in Black showed her destructive charms. Jeff Strasser launched his car into oblivion over a sand bank in turn one. Jim Hornung took to the inside groove early and had his car stall. The field — Trickle, Back, Field, Detjens, Callahan, Beyer and Marzofka — exchanged paint and when the wreckers were through, only Callahan, Beyer and Marzofka returned to action.

Jimmy Back, still running the Bob Holmes Camaro, won a 40-lap feature, and then Neil Callahan won the 50-lap season championship race. The best in the Midwest appeared to close out the year at Wausau with a Tri-R special, but the local drivers were not to be put down. Dick Trickle beat Tom Maier in the first feature. Tom Reffner beat Bob Senneker in the second. Trickle returned to defeat Tony Diane in the nightcap.

103

Friday night split the forces between LaCrosse and Capital speedways. At LaCrosse, Jim Sauter, the track champion from the year before, proved he would be hard to unseat, although Marzofka, Back and Rich Somers were determined to give it a try.

Sauter picked up two victories in May. In the second, Marzofka had the lead before losing his brakes. Detjens inherited the lead, only to have Sauter test him

Jimmy Back

on the outside several times before getting by with an inside move. Rich Somers caught Detjens for a May victory, and Jimmy Back crossed the finish line with Detjens and Marzofka rapping on his bumper in the other.

June opened with Terry Bivins making the long haul from Kansas worthwhile, as he won the Pepsi Packerland Special. Don James took an early lead in another feature that month, only to be tracked down by Pete Mahlum. Then Rich Somers, with Billy Oas in his wake, whisked by both and won convincingly. Sauter returned to the top again in July, winning three of the four events run that month. The month got off to a good start when he passed John Brevick and had clear sailing while Marzofka and Somers tried to pick their way through traffic. After battling with Back from lap 18 to 23, Sauter was on his way again. On the third evening of racing in the month, Bob Arbuckle and Pete Mahlum got crossed up, and Mahlum hit the wall hard. Jimmy Back and Rich Somers lost fenders in the action and Sauter went on to victory. Back finally stopped Sauter's drive for the points title and went into the lead himself with a clean sweep that ended the month.

Marv Marzofka got his first feature win of the year after taking the lead on lap five, but he never got to ease up because Sauter, Somers and Back followed him across the line like a pack of hungry dogs. Billy Oas won, then Back won two, but it wasn't enough. When the season was over, Jim Sauter had enough points to win the championship for a second year in a row.

The other half of the Wisconsin Rapids contingent visited Capital Speedway on Friday night and found the opponents tough. Bobby Gunn, in the course of the winter, bought Dick Trickle's 1970 Mustang and held off Ed Hume to win the opener. Billy Oas had the 22-car field looking for holes, as the green fell on the second day of action when he went sliding under the flagman sideways. Fred Bender eventually won.

Joe Shear followed that with two victories. In the first, Johnny Reimer's Nielsen-prepared Camaro fell short by half a car length. In the second, Hume and Bender fought for second under the shadow of his bumper. Dick Trickle finally got a victory, but then Shear came back with another, and Johnny Reimer went on a July rampage, winning three in a row. Shear got back on track for two more, then Larry Ninneman. Ron Marish and the modifieds sent all the late models running to the woods.

August began with Joe Shear setting a track record of 19:090, wiping out a record held by Dick Trickle and set two years previous on wide tires. Dave Watson won. Trickle won the Tri-R Dairyland 100, but, after destroying two cars the previous weekend, he had to borrow back his old Mustang from Bob Gunn. The season at

Capital closed with Trickle and Reffner splitting twin Pepsi 50's.

The central Wisconsin gang found things much more to their liking at Wisconsin Dells on Saturday night. Dick Trickle opened things with a victory when Bob Gunn lost it in the final lap and permitted Trickle to slide by on the inside. Bob Gunn found himself in second again when Larry Detjens rolled over the opposition with his hemi-powered Dodge Challenger.

Mike Miller captured a feature, but in the first Lyle Nabbefeldt Memorial 100; Trickle caught Miller on lap 31 and was gone. Minnesota drivers continued to show some punch in late June when Billy Oas won after Bob Jusola, the Flying Finn, spun.

The July Fourth weekend brought a record crowd of 6,580 to the speedway to watch Trickle and Shear each take a feature. However, Jim Back finished second twice and won the overall title. The first race took time out for a yellow when Fred Bender blew an engine and crashed into the wall. Marv Marzofka, trailing close behind, hit the wall and went for an ambulance ride to Baraboo.

Dave Field had a knack of coming on strong in the latter part of the season and 1974 proved no exception as he dusted off his 1967 Ford convertible and won in mid-July. Mike Miller sandwiched a victory between two by Jimmy Back in his 1974 Camaro. Rich Somers captured a victory in his 1972 Mustang when he got by Sauter and Harold Bahr on the inside.

Joe Shear placed second twice in the 75-lap features that highlighted the Midwest Championships and was the overall winner of the title. In the first race, Ed Howe got the victory after he slipped by Tom Reffner on lap 57. Shear finally got by Reffner with four laps to go. As the laps faded in the second race, Howe and Trickle got side by side on lap 40 and the crowd drew its breath and waited for the duel to the finish to unfold. It ended when Howe, who had just pulled ahead on lap 72, blew a tire and left the way open for Trickle.

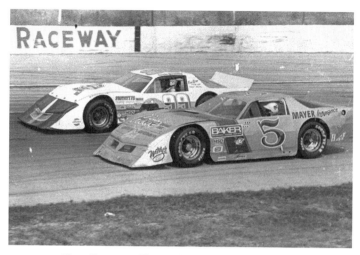

Jim Sauter (5) and Dick Trickle (99).

Bob Schmelzer took a long, thoughtful puff on his ever-present cigar and locked the gates at Columbus in 1974. By the time Schmelzer made his announcement, 11 different winners had taken the checkered at Columbus 151 Speedway. Variety, unfortunately, wasn't enough to draw crowds. Joe Shear won the final race in which the drivers gave the purse back to Schmelzer in appreciation for three years of considerate promotion.

Marv Marzofka held off Larry Detjens to win the first feature at Golden Sands to complete a sweep and dominate the show. Little did fans know things were just warming up. In the hobby race, Vic Getzloff and Joe Gaulet of Wausau crashed in turn three and bounced into the infield, where they slammed together again. Both recovered and began roaring across the infield toward the start-finish line. No sooner were they back on the track than they banged together again, finishing the race glued together at an angle, with Getzloff ahead by a thin margin. In the second race, Trickle caught Reffner and then pulled out beside him. The finish was so close a judge had to declare Reffner the winner.

Mike Miller won the next feature, but again, it was Getzloff who sent the fans home buzzing when he tried to pass six cars by taking to the inside groove. Unfortunately, all six cars were in the inside groove.

Johnny Reimer and Marv Marzofka shared twin 50's, and then Larry Detjens worked his way through traffic to win a feature that was halted by Marzofka's close brush with serious injury. Marzofka blew an engine in turn one and ended up against the retaining wall. Don Marcis spun off beside him, then Bob Abitz did a violent flip that ended up on top of Marzofka's car.

Dick Trickle got by Mike Miller on the last lap for a victory to close out the month of June, and then Dave Field provided his own fireworks of the Fourth of July weekend, as he won two 50-lap races. Neil Callahan finished second in both races.

Back moved by Marzofka. Oas downed Callahan. John Brevick surprised everyone. Callahan won as the cars stayed bunched. Back beat Callahan. Callahan came back to close the season with a double victory.

Larry Detjens won the spring opener at Kaukauna with some hard driving in the final two laps that found him passing Somers, Sauter and Miller. The "Red" race went to Shear, the "White" to Somers and the "Blue" to Reffner. Reffner finished first and second in two 104-lap events to take Kaukauna's North American Championship and then borrowed an engine to win the track's Rawhide 100.

Dick Trickle led the charge out of state with a victory at Morris, Illinois, and then he traveled to Odessa to take the Mid-American Championship.

1975
An assault
on the record

When Ed Howe sold Tom Reffner his AMC Javelin, it was like selling Dutch Schultz a machine gun. Opponents' bodies would soon be scattered all over.

The headlines at LaCrosse read like a litany. Reffner uses outside move on Detjens. Reffner moves around Shear. Reffner dominates Dr. Pepper 150. Reffner catches and passes Somers. Reffner downs Senneker. Marzofka chases Reffner in vain. Reffner roars past Paasch and scores half-lap victory. Reffner beats Trickle by fifty feet. Reffner gets victory number 55 in a runaway. Reffner wins the feature and the title.

Reffner was stopped on two occasions. On the first, his engine went bad. On the second, Jimmy Pierson spun while challenging Larry Detjens for the lead. The sliding Pierson was hit by Trickle, who bounced into Jimmy Back. Billy Oas and Reffner were both eliminated when they collided with the disabled vehicles.

In the semi-feature, Don Grant was busy destroying the opposition. Jim Bohmsach was a consistent winner. Steve Burgess, Denny Paasch, Don Marcis, and Gordie Platt also took home Wednesday night checkereds.

Thursday nights at Wausau proved to be much more difficult for the glory bound Reffner. May almost slipped by without a victory. On the first of the month, he was

Marv Marzofka, right, clowns with Tom Reffner and his crew at Kaukauna.

beaten by Trickle. Marzofka was third in a 1972 Camaro. Neil Callahan was fourth in a 1974 Nova, followed by Larry Detjens and Mike Miller, who was driving a 1970 Mustang. The second event scrambled the order, and this time it was Callahan who beat Reffner. A Mike Miller miscue in the third event set up a duel between Trickle and Reffner. Trickle held Reffner off. Reffner finally won on the last Thursday night in May and then came back to win an accident-marred feature to begin June. Reffner beat Miller after Callahan started off a chain-reaction crash involving himself, Back, Marzofka, and Trickle.

Detjens won, then Reffner's chief wrench, Pete Haferman, did some fine tuning, and Reffner closed a huge gap and sailed by Trickle for a victory. Reffner nailed down two more by passing Callahan and Back. Don Marcis and Ron Beyer put on a side-by-side duel, and then Reffner used the inside route to beat Mike Miller in a nail-biter. Neil Callahan won two in a row, and then Reffner used the inside route again to beat Bobby Allison in the "Coke 100." The season closed with victories by Back and Trickle.

The number of semi winners rivaled the listings in

the Wausau telephone directory. With the exception of John Bovee, Jim Bohmsach, and Chuck Green, no one found their way into victory lane twice. Those who made the scene once were: Rick Haase, John Zeidler, Pete Mahlum, Bob Mackesy, John Speer, Jim Hornung, Les Stankowski, Bill Voight and Ron Beyer.

By May 16 at Capital Speedway, the bounty on Reffner was $100. On June 6, Johnny Ziegler bought a new 1974 Camaro and almost collected. The bounty went up to $150. By June 27, the bounty was $200. A June 29, 100-lap special turned into a walkaway for Reffner when a broken brake caliper sent Joe Ruttman into the wall just as a duel was about to begin. On the Fourth of July, Reffner won two 50-lappers. By July 25, the bounty was $300. It was a night that saw Reffner roll his Javelin off the truck and run the three fastest laps in time trials without a warm-up.

After a 100-lap victory to begin August, Reffner experienced a drought at Capital. It was a month marked by serious accidents. It began when the throttle stuck on Tony Strupp's 1973 Camaro, and he showed the pit-men standing along the wall in turn four what the underside of his car looked like. Fans raced for cover as four posts and a section of chain link fence came crashing down on them. Strupp's airborne car came to a halt against the wall. Gary Hemmerling followed this up with a spectacular roll that earned him the honor of being the first person in the history of the track to disappear over a wall. On the same evening, Reffner, Trickle and Ziegler were giving no ground when Reffner and Trickle touched, sending Reffner head first into the second turn wall. Reffner was hospitalized overnight, and it would take a week before his car was rebuilt and back on the circuit. The Green Hornet, Ed Howe, rolled into town on August 31 and took a 100-lapper. Jim Sauter won a weekly show, then Reffner won the 100-lap season finale.

Leonard Reimer, the Ice Cream Man, would appear In the semi-feature. Alan Kulwlcki, destined for

Kaukauna fame, began to win. Old stalwarts filled out the list of semi-feature winners at Capital: Tony Strupp, Bill Retallick, Junior Dunn, Vaughn Gerke, Darrell Swartwout, Jerry Eckhardt and Wayne Erickson.

At Wisconsin Dells, Reffner opened the season by taking two 50-lap events. Then Trickle won, while Reffner fought in vain to get free of traffic. John Knaus caught Mike Waddell and then held off Tony Strupp, Larry Detjens, and Marv Marzofka. On Memorial Day weekend, Reffner scored another double victory. In the first race, Tom Maier broke the frame of his car in a violent crash. The second race was the setting for a chain-reaction wreck involving Reffner, Knaus, Leach, Marzofka and Detjens. When the smoke cleared, Reffner came back from 15 cars down to take the victory.

In June, Miller won, and then Marzofka got by a spinning Knaus to win. The month ended with Reffner and Shear each taking a 50-lap race. In the first, Trickle oiled the track. Bob Gunn slid into the wall. Joe Ruttman spun but continued. Two laps later, when the green dropped, Reffner passed Johnny Reimer and was gone.

On the Fourth of July weekend, Bob Senneker arrived with a broken leg to give lessons on the fine art of driving with an automatic transmission. First, he destroyed Jim Back's two-year-old track record with a 14:375. Then he conquered the field twice in the 50-lap races.

Reffner kept the crowd talking long into the evening the next week. Larry Detjens had already taken the white flag when Reffner got by Billy Oas. Like a rocket, Reffner was off to nose out Detjens at the finish line.

In seven days, from July 3-10, Reffner won nine features. By July 6, he had won forty features, and the fans were doing a Babe Ruth-style countdown. He was two weeks ahead of Trickle's record setting pace.

The month of August belonged to Reffner's opposition at the Dells. Johnny Ziegler won a weekly show, and then Trickle and Shear split twin 50's. Don Leach made things easier for Trickle in the first of the two events when he spun and took with him Back, Reffner,

Dick Trickle and Jim Sauter study front-end geometry at Dick's shop.

Senneker, and Howe. Reffner and Howe were done for the afternoon. In the second race, Senneker ran out of time and finished a bumper away from beating Shear. Trickle won by a car length over Johnny Ziegler, while Tom Musgrave finished third. The season closed with Howe taking the overall championship in a twin 75-lap show. In the second, Howe and Reffner flashed by Dick Trickle on lap 51 and then put on a two-man duel to the finish. Howe was not to be outclassed by his old car.

Gordie Platt won the semi-feature twice in his hometown. Reffner might be dominating the features, but no one had a stranglehold on the semi-features around the circuit. At the Dells, Mike Waddell, Steve Burgess, Bill Retallick, Rocky Breezer, Chuck Abrahams, Doug Strasburg, Dave Boodle and Richie Bickle shared the honors.

Neil Callahan won the first two features at Golden Sands, and then Tom Reffner set a track record of 13:097 and left the field behind in two 50-lap races. Callahan got an early lead and held off Reffner. Reffner came back for a sweep. Mike Miller caught Reffner and Detjens by surprise and before they could recover took the checkered. After that, nothing could stop Reffner. Each meeting put another victory in Reffner's pocket, and on August 31, he would close Golden Sands with numbers 58 and 59. Number 59 left diehard Trickle and Reffner fans arguing long into the night. Reffner finally got beside Trickle after 10 laps of hard driving and then on the last lap, the two bumped going into turn three. Trickle spun in turn four, and Reffner got the victory.

John Bovee won five semi-features. The rest were spread between Bob Mackesy, Tom Steuding, Rick Haase, Jerry Eckhardt. Chuck Abraham and Rocky Breezer. In July, nine cars tried to occupy the same spot, with the end result being the total destruction of Fluff Furo's car.

"Don't go out of town unless you are running right or the competition will blow your doors off," is Tom Reffner's philosophy. Reffner was running right in 1975 and no hometown hero could put him down. After hounding Larry Phillips from lap 48 to 71, he won the Coca-Cola 100 Memorial Day race at Odessa. In June, he took a 100-lap feature at West Chester, Ohio On July 5, he was back in Odessa to take the Firecracker 100. In September, Reffner set a track record at Grundy and won the Wayne Carter Classic.

Dick Trickle, whose Daytona efforts came to an end in a fourth lap, $15,000 accident, won the Spring Opener at Kaukauna. Johnny Ziegler won the "Red" and "Blue" segments of the main series and eventually the overall title, while Reffner won the "White" race. Reffner won a 50-lap race and the 75-lap finale at the Oktoberfest to close out the northern season and then headed south to Florida and Indiana to capture one more victory.

When Reffner ran his last race for the year in St. Petersburg, Florida, his achievements were the subject of claims and counterclaims. The dispute revolved around the Bobby Allison - Coke 100 program at Wausau. Those wire backed the theory that he had tied Trickle's record of 67 victories held that the two 25-lap races that preceded the 50-lap main event were simply

Tom Reffner is all smiles after a good night at Capital Super Speedway.

preliminary events and not features. Proponents of a new short-track record for Reffner held that the only way one could come up with 100 laps of feature racing, as the event was billed, was if the two 25-lap races were also features. When all was over, it was declared a tie.

When Tom Reffner tied Dick Trickle's record for short track victories in a season he took a great deal of pride in the fact that it was in an American Motors product. Tom has always taken pride in taking an off-brand and making it a winner. As he reflects on his career, it was advanced by having Pete Haferman as mechanic from 1974 to 1978, the purchase of the AMC from Ed Howe, and having Superamerica as a sponsor. Among his victories, he cherishes the World Cup 400 at Kansas City in 1976. It paid over $10.000 to win. His worst crash came at I-70 in 1972 when a ball joint broke, triggering a wreck that would leave him with broken ribs. Close behind in severity was a wreck at Elko, Minnesota, in which he was knocked unconscious.

1976
A rising star

Mike Miller began his career in Minnesota, then moved to Wisconsin Rapids to race against some of the finest short track drivers in the United States.

It all began at Elko, Minnesota, where the moments before his first race were filled with terror. Previous to his first race, he had been working in an outboard motor repair shop. Gas, accidently spilled, had ignited and burned his whole right side. As he approached his first race, the fear of fire possessed him. Prior to the race, he took off his watch and ring so that when the blaze he expected started, at least those items wouldn't be melted. His foot bounced nervously on the gas pedal, but there was no way out that wouldn't cause embarrassment.

Once the race started, Miller calmed down and finished well. From that evening on, he conquered one goal after another. In 1976, Miller's Mil-lir Mustang would begin to win consistently on the tough Wisconsin circuit.

A new promoter, Paul Kaczrowski, took over at Golden Sands and Joe Shear nipped Johnny Ziegler in the Tuesday night opener. On the second Tuesday night, Mike Miller beat Marzofka by a quarter of a lap. He proved that he was a force to be dealt with at the next program when, after a collision between Billy Voight and Tom Reffner tightened the pack, he roared past the leaders to victory. Johnny Ziegler won a "Spirit of '76" feature and then Mike Miller came back the next week to soundly defeat Rich Somers and the field. Then, on successive evenings, he beat Reffner, Trickle, Somers and Back. The point was made. A $50 bounty was offered to stop him. Glory can be fleeting, and Jimmy Back proved it when he snapped up the bounty on the very next outing.

Miller would finish as high-point man at the track, but the rest of the season was stingy on victories. Reffner won three in a row, including another "Spirit of '76" race and was in contention for a fourth until he became involved in an accident.

Mike Miller

Marv Marzofka had Reffner on his bumper and Trickle on his outside door when Trickle tapped Marzofka. Marzofka's Camaro and Reffner's Javelin spun, and Trickle went on to victory. Reffner came back to win two more, one of them the "Spirit of '76 III." Then, Larry Detjens switched to a Camaro and beat Reffner and Miller. Trickle won when Miller's ignition failed, and then Jim Bohmsach took the final feature of the year.

Dave Watson won LaCrosse's Wednesday night opener, and then Mark Lamoreaux did a superb job of holding off a last-lap charge by Dick Trickle to take the second feature. The final race of May left Mike Miller a fatigued, but proud winner. First, Ted Kitzman and Dave Watson took turns running beside him. Both faded. Then Rich Somers moved alongside for still another failing bid for the lead.

June found Tom Reffner seated in a new 1974 Javelin, and he was quick to demonstrate its capabilities. While Bob Senneker won one of the 50-lap events in the Dr. Pepper 150, Reffner won the opener and the finale. He won another feature, and then Mike Miller beat him across the line. Reffner came back on the next evening of racing with a clean sweep and then followed that up with a record, 20.345, and a feature win on Bobby Allison Night. Reffner won three more features, including one that saw Dave Watson make up a full straightaway, only to get nosed out in the final ten feet.

A three-car wreck, triggered by Jim Sauter's exploding radiator, caused Reffner to watch Trickle win from the sidelines, but Reffner was first to the flag one week

later. Billy Oas surprised everyone with a victory and then surprised a trailing Tom Reffner by blowing an engine and oiling the track. Reffner and Don Grant ended up against the wall, and Dick Trickle went on to hold off Lamoreaux for the win. Reffner sandwiched a victory in between two by Larry Detjens to close out the season.

Bruce Giebels congratulates Marv Marzofka at Wisconsin Dells.

Larry Anderson dominated semi-feature action against hard running veterans Jim Weber, Ralph Bakewell, Curt Iverson, Don Grant, Bob Mackesy, Jim Johnson, Don Turner and John Brevick.

No one liked going to Wausau as much as Tom Reffner did in 1976. By August 5, he had won 12 races there. Dick Trickle and Mike Miller were double winners and Marv Marzofka and Jim Bohmsach carried the checkered once.

Roy Bohm was the man to beat in the semi-feature, and if he was beaten, it was usually by Fluff Furo, Billy Voight, John Bovee or Larry Sparks.

Capital Speedway took on a southern Wisconsin atmosphere, as Johnny Ziegler and Dave Watson threw their weight around on Friday nights. Watson couldn't catch Ziegler on opening day, but he did come back on the next Sunday afternoon to steer through a multi-car accident and beat Joe Shear out by the width of the finish line.

Ziegler finished fourth, behind Reffner. Then Ziegler won, while Watson, Shear, Trickle, and Sauter fought for second. In the next race, Watson edged Shear, and Ziegler came back to set a track record of 18.884 and win two features. Ziegler was awarded another victory when Tom Reffner was disqualified for loading up and refusing to let anyone tear his engine down. Randy Sweet won a 76-lap Fourth of July special, and then Dave Watson won three features in a row. On one of the evenings, Johnny Ziegler sat it out while Janet Guthrie drove his car. Following the late-season pattern, Tom Reffner took the first feature and the finale in the Badger 150, and then Larry Detjens took the closing race of the season in his Camaro.

In one of the worst accidents of the year, Dick Trickle destroyed a new Ford Granada in turn three. "The car was handling real well, so I took it down deep into the corner. Backing out of it, I naturally shoved on the brake. When I heard the roar of the motor continue to build, I shoved the brake harder; but it just started the front wheels sliding and I had a hard time holding the steering wheel. It wanted to go up into the wall at a direct angle, and I had to hang on hard to bring it around as much as I could. With both hands struggling, I couldn't get to the key in time. I guess I didn't do a good job of steering or of reaching the key. Just as I got to the wall, I wondered if it was a little too much this time. The next thing I knew, the car was upside down and sliding on its roof. Sparks were flying everywhere, and

Mike Miller gets caught going the wrong way on a one-way street.

gas and oil were dripping down. My first instinct was to get out of there and away from the car before it started on fire." A badly shaken Trickle escaped without injury.

Mike Miller enjoyed racing at Wisconsin Dells and took five features in the course of the summer. Johnny Ziegler took the opener in his 1975 Firebird but failed in a last-lap attempt to beat Jim Sauter in the Lyle Nabbefeldt Memorial race. June began with Bob Senneker dominating a twin fifty program that found Ziegler's chances smashed against the wall after Somers and Watson spun ahead of him. Shear held off Miller to win, and then Bobby Gunn fired up his 1970 Mustang museum piece for two victories in a row. Reffner and Marzofka won, and then Miller ran off three victories in a row. It was Reffner and then Miller again before Joe Shear dominated the latter weeks of the season. Rocky Breezer was the favorite in the Dells semi-features.

As the season ended, Larry Detjens gathered momentum and took the Minnesota Fair 400 in his 1974 Camaro.

MARV MARZOFKA

Mighty Moose

It was early morning, and Marv Marzofka was on his way to work at Johnson's AMC when he first spotted the buck. The lovesick fellow was trying to make his way through a chain link fence to the doe on the other side and had his antlers hooked in the fence. The taste of fresh venison was in Marv's mouth by the time he got to work, and it wasn't long before he had convinced another mechanic to go back to the scene with him. "I'll grab the deer and you stab him."

Marv Marzofka

Marv grabbed the deer, but the deer pulled free and took off through a patch of saplings with Marv on his back. While the saplings whipped Marv, the worst was yet to come. When the buck finally collapsed, it chose a bed of sand burrs to land in. One of the greatest wrestling matches in central Wisconsin followed and Marv began to resemble a pincushion. Finally, both Marv and the deer lay in exhaustion, neither able to move.

By this time, Marv's friend had caught up. "Stab him." Marv whispered.

"I can't. I left the knife back at the car!"

The deer got up and ran off.

Deer never treat Marv Marzofka with respect. The

121

reason can be found in an old Indian legend told by an aged man in a woodside tavern near Babcock. Since locals have accused the proprietress of watering down the drinks, there is even more reason to believe the story the man tells.

According to the legend, the first people of the universe lived above the sky and there was no earth. When the citizens of this kingdom decided one day to dig up a tree, it fell through the hole they had dug and disappeared. As the people gazed through the hole they had created in the sky, they saw nothing but a vast expanse of water below. Through the purity of the water, they could see the earth. They decided to dive for it and bring some of it up and place it on the back of a giant turtle, thus creating an island where they could live. First Otter, then Muskrat and Duck dove. The depths were too great and they all died. Then Mighty Moose tried. He brought back a mouthful of earth and spit it upon the back of the turtle, creating the great cranberry bog west of Babcock. He became the hero and all the deer in Wisconsin envied this Mighty Moose. Maiden deer swooned over him.

But years passed by and the white man came to Wisconsin. According to the belief of the ancients, to know the name of a person was to have a certain power over that person. We can only guess the consequences of being able to paint a picture and make an exact replica of a person. Yet, this is what happened. A Chevrolet dealer in Black River Falls named Moose Peterson decided to paint a moose on the side of the cars he sponsored. The spirit of the most majestic of all animals, Mighty Moose, creator of the cranberry bogs, had been captured therein.

Mighty Moose could only struggle against his captors. In the very first race that Marv ran for Peterson at Stratford, Moose's spirit sent the car spinning out of control and sailing backwards into the railroad tie wall that protected the grandstands. The impact shortened the car by about four feet and wrinkled Mighty Moose's

Jim Sauter (7) and Marv Marzofka (91).

face.

Marv thought he would be fired as a driver. Fate smiled, and Marzofka was to continue as the young driver of car No. 91. A savage beating was required to straighten the Moose's face. Mighty Moose, his forehead still smarting from the beating, decided his best avenue of escape was to play along with the game. Soon, the Moose enjoyed his new role. He loved carrying the Ridge Runner home to victory and receiving the accolades of the roaring crowd. He loved the parties afterwards. As the summer progressed, his portrayer indicated this by making his eyes more bloodshot.

As time progressed, the Moose began to change from the Spirit of Blessing who had created the cranberry bogs to a cruel Trickster. 'Tis a cruel game riding on the door of a stock car and only the meanest survive. Once the captor of his spirit, Peterson himself, rolled a '56 Chevy with the Moose's image upon it in a most violent manner on the fourth turn at Adams-Friendship Speedway. While Peterson hung upside down in his seat belts, fearful of the fall when he would release them, poor Moose suffered having his antlers and chin scraped away, to say nothing of the dirt in his eyes.

The most fearful assaults were to come from Nelson Drinkwine, who insisted upon using the inner groove of the track and often roared full power into the side of any outside passerby. In those days, the exhaust pipes stuck out over the front tire at ear level to the person in the next car. If Marzofka can still remember the exhaust of Drinkwine's car, front tight to his side, burning his whiskers right off, and the sound rattling every bone in his head, think of the Moose on the door with a tire rubbing angrily at his chin. At one point, Drinkwine pushed the passing Marzofka off the track three races in a row. The Moose grew vindictive and tough.

One day, the Spirit of Earth challenged him with the idea of knowing someone who could defeat him. Mighty Moose would not listen, but he still followed the Spirit of Earth to a spot in the cranberry bogs where she placed a child before him and commanded him to make the child walk and talk. Moose sang. The child laughed. The Moose walked upright on his hind legs. The child smiled. Moose grew angry and yelled. The child cried but would not walk or talk. Moose knew that he had been defeated. He was banished to a spot below the bogs as his punishment.

His last act before departing was to tell all the does that if one could successfully kiss his ghostly image on the passing yellow truck of Marv Marzofka, it would become the fairest of all the deer, and Moose, handsome brute that he was, would come back and marry that deer. He cautioned the bucks never to reveal their names to Marzofka and promised that if one could bring the truck to a halt with its antlers, he would give that buck his many powers.

And, so the deer in central Wisconsin refuse to give Marzofka respect. They slam against his hauler as he travels through the cranberry bogs on his way to LaCrosse Interstate Speedway with such frequency that Marv's insurance adjuster cries when the phone rings. And bucks win wrestling matches by not revealing their names. Moose will have his revenge.

1977
Firechicken

The season started out with Dick Trickle driving a very familiar 1970 Mustang. Then, on May 15, at Kaukauna, he debuted a still-to-be-lettered 1977 Firebird. Once again, the feature victory count was on. An indication of how the odds were stacked against the Mustang can be seen in the LaCrosse opener. Tom Reffner swept the event. In the feature, the gap between Reffner and Trickle was closed when Steve Arndt blew an engine and brought out the yellow. When the green fell again, it took Reffner just one lap to get by Trickle.

Marzofka managed to hold off the three-day-old Firebird on the next night of racing at LaCrosse, but then Trickle got two in a row at LaCrosse. In the second, Reffner followed him through the pack, but couldn't gather enough steam to get close to the White Knight.

Bob Senneker came to town and won both ends of the Dr. Pepper show. Marzofka finished second in both races, and Trickle looked strong until he blew in the first feature. Marzofka won, and then Trickle turned on the power. He got Marzofka on lap 10 the next evening and then erased Miller's straightaway lead to win the race. Ralph Bakewell and Don Grant collided coming out of turn four on the final lap the next evening. The action was already over for Mike Miller, who had successfully held off Steve Burgess for the victory, but it was just beginning for Bakewell. His Javelin tore out three sections of the infield guard rail and then sailed 20 feet before coming to a rest in turn one.

Marzofka and Reffner took the features while Sauter got the overall title in the Fourth of July Uncola Special. In the first race, Jim Johnson took an early lead. Marzofka lost no time in moving into second ahead of Jeff Stegemeyer. It took him a half-lap to pass Johnson when the green came out after a Butch Miller spin. In the second race, a sizeable Pete Mahlum lead disappeared when Steve Arndt spun and Tom Reffner drew into striking distance.

Jeff Stegemeyer had the early lead on July 6. He was passed by Mike Miller, who in turn was passed by Trickle and Reffner, who stayed glued to the Firebird's bumper to the end. Trickle dominated July and by August 3 he had victory number 44.

Mike Miller found the going easier when a four-car crash eliminated top competitors like Burgess and Sauter. At the end, though, Tom Reffner was still around to make things tough. Reffner came back to win two features and then Steve Burgess drove through a multi-car crash to take the final weekly show.

Burgess came within one car of an Oktoberfest victory. Rich Somers led the first 19 laps. Then Miller took over and led until lap 33. Sauter was challenging for the lead when he blew a tire and went into the wall. Racing slowed again when Trickle blew a tire. When racing resumed, Larry Detjens moved by Miller, and Burgess closed in to apply pressure for the last 11 laps. Extra power on the straights gave Detjens the victory.

Greg Holzhausen and Jim Johnson flexed a lot of muscle in the semi-feature. Also coming out on top were Orv Buelow, Don Grant, John Speer, Bob Lee, LaVerne Grandall and John Brevick.

At Wausau, Larry Detjens hovered in the shadow of victory all season. He won the opener by catching Reffner in the last lap. The second feature event was a carbon copy with Mike Miller the victim. Marv Marzofka held Detjens off in the third feature and then Trickle narrowly defeated Larry after racing side-by-side with him for 17 laps. Detjens was not to be denied the next night out. He broke out of the pack and caught Reffner with one lap to go.

Bobby Allison used to say that each time he came to Wisconsin, he was taught a lesson in short track racing. Allison was a regular competitor at state tracks.

Trickle won when he got an early lead and Detjens ran out of time. Then Jim Bohmsach managed to finish a bumper length ahead of Detjens. June came to an end with a Detjens victory. Orv Buelow took the early lead. Trickle challenged him and then dropped out with a clogged fuel filter. Detjens picked his way through traffic and finally passed Buelow on lap 25.

Although Detjens was always near at the finish, Dick Trickle dominated the remainder of the season at Wausau. He began July by passing Larry on lap 15. He and Tom Steuding split the mid-season twin 30-lap events. Trickle went on to win three more features. In the final one of the season, his throttle stuck and he brought the car around to the checkered by delicate manipulation of clutch and key. Familiar faces carried the flag in the semi-feature: Gary Porter, Ron Beyer, Al Schultz, Roy Schmidke, Don Marcis, Les Stankowski and Bob Mackesy.

Tom Reffner got off to a flying start at Capital Speedway on Friday nights. On April 30, he was the first repeat victor when he passed Larry Detjens after a three-lap duel in the middle of the race. Detjens won the next Friday night, and then Reffner came back to hold off repeated challenges by Joe Shear and Jimmy Pierson.

The season soured on Reffner's Bemco-built Hornet and Trickle found new life when he brought his Firebird to Capital Speedway. He beat Joe Shear in a come-from-behind victory and then went on to sweep two more programs. Fred Bender and Larry Detjens won, then Tom Reffner switched back to his 1974 Javelin and again found himself in victory lane. Good luck abandoned the Blue Knight the next evening and he blew an engine, taking Steve Burgess and Bender into the wall with him. Trickle exchanged leads with Shear and then pulled away on the final lap.

Trickle came out on top in a four-lap duel with Steve Burgess, then Larry Detjens made it look easy when he defeated Tom Reffner by a half-lap. Mike Miller won the final race in August, and when the crowd gathered for a final time in September, Trickle got two victories and Tom Reffner one in the Capital City 150.

The season started in controversy at Wisconsin Dells when promoter Larry Wehrs installed a two-barrel carburetor rule. Jimmy Back, Jim Sauter and Marv Marzofka made the switch and dominated the first four shows, but there just weren't enough cars to make it a worthwhile venture. As a result, the track switched back to Central Wisconsin Racing Association rules in hopes of luring back such drivers as Dick Trickle, Tom Reffner and Larry Detjens.

The Dells began its second season with a battle between Marzofka and Trickle for feature honors. Miller came up to challenge Marzofka on the outside but could never get far enough ahead to drop down in front. They went around on lap 11 even and stayed that way until they drove under the checkered, with Marzofka inches ahead.

The next week, Joe Shear made his debut in a new Fred Nielsen Camaro, set a record 14:247 and then went on to pass Jimmy Pierson on lap 10 in the feature and never was challenged. It was Shear again the next week, then Bobby Gunn got some help from a pack of slower cars that held everyone back while he built a substantial lead. Cal Wilhelm spun in the consolation race coming out of turn four. Al Conant powered into the driver's side of Wilhelm's disabled vehicle and there was a long delay while Wilhelm, suffering from a broken leg, was taken out of the twisted wreckage. Dave Watson beat Shear in the next program by a half car length and then Dick Trickle came back to take both of the Lyle Nabbefeldt Memorial features.

Jim Sauter took a victory away from Mike Miller, then Jimmy Back demonstrated how cool and controlled drivers can be. His car came loose coming out of turn four in the heat race and rode the wall in a shower of sparks the full length of the front straight. By careful control of the throttle, Back kept the damage limited to a bumper that was ground away and came back to win the feature.

Steve Burgess got the lead on lap four in the first feature to be run in July. Then, Denny Paasch got off to a good lead while everyone else was trying to get around Arnie Christen and Rocky Breezer. Finally, Joe Shear broke through and went on to pass Paasch on lap 16. In the next feature, Rocky Breezer and Bob Ford brought out the red flag on lap three in an accident that took most of the field with them. When racing resumed, Tom Reffner quickly disposed of Musgrave on Lap 11 and moved on to victory. Marv Marzofka closed out the month by going from the back to the front.

New faces took the top three places on the first Saturday in August: Richie Bickle, Jim Hornung and Ted Musgrave. Joe Shear won the 75-lap Dave Marcis Night special. The following Saturday night, Tom Reffner just got ahead of Jeff Stegemeyer with two laps left. Reffner looked like a sure winner in the 100-lap finale, and then his tires gave out. Mike Miller came charging down on him to win the race. Dick Trickle and Larry Detjens drove side by side for the last 10 laps, with Trickle gaining the upper hand and taking second place.

By June 14, Tom Reffner had nailed down victory number four at Golden Sands. Trickle had won, and in every instance, Larry Detjens had to content himself with a second-place finish. Detjens' fate remained the same on June 21 when Mike Miller brought his 1970 Mustang home first and Larry had to scurry to get around Reffner and finish second.

Dick Trickle won both of the 50-lap races held on the Fourth of July weekend. In the first, he passed Tom Reffner for the lead on lap 21 and, in the second, he took the lead on lap 13. In the next program, Trickle and Miller had everyone standing for a better view, as they ran next to each other until the final lap, when Trickle got behind a slower car and Miller used that advantage to take the lead. The two shared 50-lap victories the next week. In the first race, Les Stankowski led un-

Jim Bohmsach gave up driving to become Dick Trickle's head wrench.

til Fluff Furo caught him in his 1974 Barracuda. Jimmy Back caught Furo and then Tom Reffner caught Back. On lap 39, Mike Miller passed Reffner. Roy Schmidke led the second race for 10 laps in his 1972 Nova. Marv Marzofka passed him and then Trickle passed Marzofka for the lead on lap 28. In the two races that followed, Jim Bohmsach found himself coming up short twice, once to Tom Reffner and another time to Jim Sauter.

Roy Schmidtke found himself on the receiving end

of a lot of pain when the throttle stuck at the drop of the green on a feature race at Golden Sands and his car shot off the first turn, hitting the retaining wall. "It felt like every bone in my body was at its breaking point. I didn't know a chest could be technicolor, but the next morning, mine was green, blue, yellow, and every other imaginable color."

Bob Mackesy dominated semi-feature action at Golden Sands, and when he wasn't carrying off the checkered, the honors went to Dave Boodle. Les Stankowski, Orv Buelow, Larry Baumel, Don Marcis or Bill Voight.

Dick Trickle made the switch from Ford to Firebird on a sunny afternoon in May at Kaukauna and good fortune smiled upon the car immediately as he beat Jimmy Pierson by a car length in the spring opener. Trickle's luck held through the Red and White races. In the Red race, he easily defeated Larry Detjens. The White race started with Fred Bender taking an early lead, only to be passed by Joe Shear, who ran away from the field. A Bob Abitz spin brought him back to within striking distance and he soon found Dick Trickle bumping on his door. The yellow came out when Bender's engine exploded in flames. Trickle narrowly won the dash to the finish with Shear.

ARTGO Racing came to Capital Speedway on May 30 and Joe Shear and Ed Howe shared 50-lap victories. Howe led for two laps in the first race before Shear took over and then came back in the nightcap to slip by Larry Phillips four laps from the end for a victory of his own. ARTGO was back at Capital on Father's Day and Dick Trickle took a 50-lap event and the 100-lap finale. In the finale, only Larry Detjens managed to stay in the same lap with Trickle. Mark Martin made his debut in Wisconsin and finished behind Larry Schuler in the remaining 50-lap race. In the second half of the Father's Day program at Grundy, Larry Detjens withstood the challenges of Trickle to score a victory of his own. The next time ARTGO came to Capital, Bob Senneker won two

50-lap events and Trickle one. In the Summer Nationals, Detjens and Senneker each took a 75-lap feature at Capital Speedway, and then everyone traveled to Grundy, where Larry Phillips took the Wayne Carter 100.

The 1972 Nova had gone from the glory of being driven to a USAC victory at Kaukauna by Dave Marcis to the everyday existence of short-track racing at Tomahawk before Dave Deppe, the car's original owner, spent a long evening drinking and talking about the virtues of the car with its present owner, Chuck Abraham. Before the last beer was drunk, the car was back in the hands of its first lover. At three o'clock in the morning, Mrs. Deppe looked out the window and whispered, "I don't believe it. I don't believe you did it!" After the car had been stripped to its roll cage, it was rebuilt into a 1977 Skylark that would dominate the Milwaukee USAC show. With Dave Watson behind the wheel, the car won two races and three pole positions.

Odessa proved to be a favorite of Wisconsin drivers. In May, Dick Trickle ran the 300-lap ASA show. He returned in July and again turned Joe Shear into a runner-up in temperatures that stood at over 100 degrees. "The spectators almost collapsed watching the race," Trickle said afterward "About 50 laps from the end, I thought I had had it. It took me about three weeks to recover." Joe Shear said, "It took me about 15 minutes to get my bearings. It was so hot that it was almost impossible to hold on to the steering wheel." In September, Larry Detjens came on strong to beat Bob Senneker in the World Cup 400.

In still more out-of-state action, Dick Trickle traveled to Cincinnati to win the Queen City Benefit in front of Dave Marcis, Junior Hanley and Dave Watson. In October, Tom Reffner found the west to his liking, capturing the Coke 150 at Colorado Springs.

RICH SOMERS

Somers known for smooth driving

While he hasn't grabbed as much of the spotlight as Dick Trickle, Tom Reffner, or Jimmy Back, Rich Somers has carved his own spot in the history of central Wisconsin racing.

To think of Somers is to think of a smooth driving style, immaculately prepared cars, and a family that follows him wherever he goes. His father, Felix, has been his mechanic since he started racing. His wife, Ann, has been with him from the start. "I have only missed two of his races," says Ann. "One night our son, Rick, had a temperature of 104. Rich won at the Dells. I was really mad, but what could I do."

Rich Somers

When Rich was a child his father worked at the Polonia Service Garage. Rich watched his father and slowly fell in love with automobiles. As he grew up he traveled to Wisconsin Rapids' Griffith Park and the track where all of the present day veterans got their start, Stratford Speedway.

It was while he was enjoying a date with his fiancée, Ann, at Griffith Park that a friend, Ron Gagas, offered him an opportunity to drive. The seed was planted and four years later he would bring home his first car, a 1956 Ford owned by James Firkus. With a family to sup-

133

port, Somers had little money to use for racing and Firkus would be instrumental in keeping him in a race car during the early part of his career. Firkus owned a salvage yard in Plover, Wisconsin, and had a ready supply of parts at hand. He would supply the car and equipment if Rich and Felix would work on the car.

"The beginning was a lot of work," says Rich. "We spent a lot of time experimenting. There wasn't much success or glory. We'd try this rear end and then that. We'd try this offset with that axle and another with that one. It seems as though I must have made a hundred wheels." The car won one race in 1963, a third heat at Griffith Park.

In 1964 Firkus and Somers built a 1958 Ford which they nicknamed "Lil Thumper". Somers moved up to the feature but four years of racing on dirt and asphalt brought few victories. "I don't consider myself a hard charger like Dick Trickle or Tom Reffner," says Somers. "I just like to run — be there the next day without having to work on the car, because I have another job to tend to in the daytime. Some people who watch racing think the way to win a race is purely by power. But I think the biggest thing is making it through that next turn without slipping or fishtailing, because you're then going that much faster coming down the straightaway."

That smooth racing style that he developed in his early days paid off with his first feature victory in June 1965. He would not win a feature again until the close of 1966 and the Labor Day races at Marathon Park in Wausau and Marshfield Fairgrounds. He won two features on the dirt at Wausau and another on the dirt at Marshfield. Then he switched to the asphalt and closed out the season with a victory at Golden Sands Speedway.

At the end of the 1968 season, Firkus and Somers parted ways. Somers would sum up the six year partnership in these words, "It's funny, my car has to feel good — if the car isn't to my liking I don't go that hard. I push to the safe, sensible limit. With either of the first

Rich Somers (15) moves ahead of Jerry Eckhardt (61).

two cars I never felt that confident. The only place the straight axle worked was on the dirt and the 1958 never felt good except on the dirt. Toward the end, Firkus always had guys coming in and telling him how to do it. He probably had a lot of people telling him he had the best of cars but not the best of drivers."

In 1969 Somers bought an ex-Sam McQuagg 1964 Mercury and raced at Kaukauna in a special class of cars that favored IMCA rules. He ran a few IMCA races but concentrated on Kaukauna where he has the distinction of being the first and last Grand National champion. Drivers were not willing to build cars for a night's racing each week and the division collapsed.

In 1970 he changed the car over to a short-track Torino and ran selected races at Kaukauna, Oregon and LaCrosse. The car wasn't a winner and Somers struggled until 1973 when he gambled and had Bemco

Engineering build a 1973 Mustang. "I was shocked when he built a house the year before," says Ann, "and then he bought the Bemco. Sometimes he just does things, like when he decided to race to begin with, but it works out. After 10 years of racing he had a $12,000 dream machine." The second week out he won the feature at Kaukauna. He won at Kaukauna again the next week. He finished the season with 14 feature victories and a fourth place finish at the Minnesota State Fair.

In 1974 he won seven features, again finished fourth at the Minnesota State Fair, and won the Red, White, and Blue Series at Kaukauna. He also won the Santa Rosa rematch at Wisconsin Dells with Joe Shear chasing him all the way. In 1975 he continued to follow the same circuit— Golden Sands, Kaukauna, LaCrosse and Madison.

It was during this period of time that he quit his job at Copp's Distributors, his sponsor since the purchase of the dream machine, and bought a supper club near Minocqua. A non-race related accident in which he broke both of his ankles plus the duties of running his own restaurant often kept him from racing a great deal. From 1980 to 1982, he raced on his night off at Kaukauna.

In 1982 he sold the restaurant and moved back to Stevens Point and went to work for Mengel Redi Mix. He suffered through some hard times in the 1980's. "I haven't had enough chassis to be competitive. I've only had five since I started racing and that is close to 25 years ago. Maybe that is the reason I am still in it. If I had bought one each year, I would probably have gone broke by now."

Top-of-the-line chassis or not, Somers was still a top-flight competitor. In 1986 he was third in points at Slinger in a tight race with Al Schill and Conrad Morgan. In 1987 he would lead one of the Slinger National events until forced out with mechanical problems.

1978
Marv is marvelous

Marv Marzofka was a race driver, but he also loved fishing and hunting with his three sons. He once bought a boat for fishing on Lake Michigan and he and his sons would often rush home from there to race at Wisconsin Dells on a Saturday night. In the fall, he and the boys would first bow hunt and then spend the gun season at City Point.

"I thought it was great to be champion at all the tracks I raced at — Wausau, LaCrosse, Wisconsin Dells, Golden Sands." Marzofka could say in retrospect. "It was super. Everyone has something they have done. Dick and Tom have won 67 features in a year. Some win big races. My goal was to be champion at all the tracks I raced at."

At LaCrosse, the season got underway with Tom Reffner holding off Rich Somers in his 1978 Concord. Jim Sauter, Steve Burgess and Larry Detjens battled for third place awards. The second night, Steve Burgess made up a straightaway on Marzofka and Somers and took the honors.

Bobby Allison came for a special night, but the locals did most of the serious racing. Mike Miller had to struggle to take the lead from Sauter on lap 21. His worries weren't over, as Dick Trickle moved in to apply the pressure.

The overall title in the Dr. Pepper show went to Larry Detjens, who finished first in one 50-lapper and third in the other. Dick Trickle took to the torch after a first-race crash and put things back together in time to win the second race. The action got started when Tom

137

Reffner moved to the outside in an effort to pass Trickle on lap 10. As the pair fought it out on a turn, they touched and both went into the wall. Reffner was out for the day. It was a bitter pill to swallow because he had won the two weeks previous to that, edging Burgess one week and outrunning Trickle the next.

After the Dr. Pepper series, June belonged to Mike Miller and his 1978 Cutlass. He beat Marzofka's 1978 Camaro. Then, he finished four car lengths ahead of Larry Detjens. Finally, he came back to beat Marzofka again.

Marzofka turned the tables on Miller to begin July and left him watching Bill Gronley wave the checkered from a distance. Then, Trickle got hot and won four features before Marzofka could jump back in the winner's circle. He narrowly defeated Marzofka in one race and then put on a side-by-side duel with Marzofka that found him losing control but winning when Marzofka backed out of it to avoid trouble. Marzofka edged Reffner and then came back the next week for a sweep. Tom Reffner got his revenge and liked it so much he came back to win the final event of the year. The race started with Mike Miller passing Trickle, who was hurting from a crash in Indiana, for the lead. It didn't take long, however, before Reffner swept by Miller.

Semi-feature action at LaCrosse found a blend of the old and the new. LaVerne Grandall, Don Turner and Orv Buelow dominated a field of winners that included Denny Paasch, Jim Johnson, Steve Moll, Don Grant and Greg Holzhausen.

Larry Detjens got things started at his home track with a clean sweep. Miller beat Marzofka by a couple of feet, and then Detjens returned to earn a hard-fought victory. First, he had to battle with Tom Reffner for half the race and then, when Reffner faded, Dick Trickle moved in to finish second.

Lady Luck was on Mike Miller's side in mid-June when he found himself out in front with a right rear tire going flat. Fortunately, time ran out before Trickle, Marzofka or Detjens could do anything about it. Marzofka overcame Trickle twice, and then Miller debuted a new Cutlass and took the mid-season championship race. August began with Marzofka again beating Trickle. Then Mike Miller and Tom Reffner put on a nine-lap duel in which Miller emerged victorious. Reffner came back to beat Back and Miller in a race that was stopped when

Marv Marzofka, the Ridge Runner, had Moose Peterson's sponsorship for many years. In the early days, Marv and Evert Fox drove 1957 yellow Chevrolets. Later, Marv drove a Camaro. Sometimes, the motors came out of cars on Moose's showroom floor.

Jim Hornung and Dick Trickle went over the sand bank in turn one. On Fan Appreciation Night, it took local favorite Larry Detjens until the last lap to get a slight advantage over Mike Miller. The car slid and then he recovered to win the race.

In the track's final race of the season, Miller's crew worked until the green was about to fall before getting a new engine installed. Miller responded by driving hard for 100 laps and just getting by Detjens. But as at LaCrosse, when the dust settled and the points were counted, it was Marzofka who was track champion.

Capital Speedway suffered from lack of attendance. It opened, and Dick Trickle dominated the action. It closed and then opened again in mid-August.

When the season was over at Wisconsin Dells, everyone sang a verse of "Rainy Day People." A number of programs were cancelled and Marv Marzofka was declared the winner in two rain-shortened shows. Mike Miller got credit in another without ever having to run a lap.

When the season finally got underway on May 20, Dick Trickle and Marv Marzofka patiently spent 20 laps getting through traffic and then battled for four laps before Marzofka was forced to lift his foot when he got stuck behind some slower cars. Ron Bakeberg spun and both Doc Herold and Gary Porter ended up going into the wall with him in the first heat.

Jimmy Back arrived late with his 1974 Camaro but was still too much for Marzofka. Dick Trickle won his favorite races, the Lyle Nabbefeldt twin 55's. In the first, he passed Mike Miller on lap 24. Then John Burbridge and Mike Miller tangled, and Larry Detjens ended up in the wall. On lap 31, Rocky Breezer blew and the yellow flag closed the gap between Marzofka and Trickle. They struggled for 12 laps before Trickle got the upper hand. In the second heat race, it took 29 laps for Trickle to work his way up to third. Two laps later, he caught Rich Somers, then on lap 29, he took the lead from Mike Miller.

Trickle's car didn't always look this sharp. Once Marlin Walbeck told him to paint the hood or he, Walbeck, would paint it for him. Walbeck ended up painting it green and it stayed that way the rest of the summer.

Things didn't go as well for Trickle on the next outing. The spirit was there, but several attempts on the outside still found him a half car length short of overcoming Marzofka at the checkered flag.

July began with Marzofka inheriting the lead from Trickle's badly smoking Firebird. It wasn't an easy victory, though, for Mike Miller soon caught him. The two were even going down the back straight, and it turned out to be a narrow win for Marzofka.

The next night out, Jimmy Back left Trickle and Marzofka fighting for second and Reffner buried behind a slower car. Next, Steve Burgess used a 1978 Camaro to catch Ron Beyer on lap 14 and go on uncontested. John Knaus had the early lead on Dave Marcis Night, but Miller and Marzofka got by and finished in that order. Pat Schauer got the lead early in the mid-season championships. Steve Burgess caught him. Mike Miller passed the pair and used them as a buffer to build a lead. Shear finally got by and narrowed the lead to a car length with three laps to go. Shear tried the outside route around Miller on lap 48, then backed off and tried the inside before defeating Miller by inches. Steve Holzhausen got the first feature victory of his career in August when he grabbed the lead from A.J. Anderson on lap six. In September, while everyone else was at the Minnesota Fair, Jimmy Back slipped back into town to pick up some pin money. Marv Marzofka didn't record a lot of firsts, but he turned consistent driving into another title at the Dells.

Golden Sands was the fourth of Marzofka's championships. Trickle held him off, and then Marzofka won two in a row, easily defeating Larry Detjens in the second. Trickle defeated Miller and Reffner, then Miller came back to get Trickle. Trickle won the mid-season championships after making up a half-lap on Marzofka. Marzofka beat Back, then Back came on strong to leave Miller and Marzofka in his wake. Again, Marzofka wrapped up the championship.

Vic Getzloff was a driver, tire changer and member of Dick Trickle's crew.

"Wausau proved to be the toughest," Marzofka said after the season. "I had to drop out of the final feature and ended up winning the title by seven points. It was a super year. Nothing broke until toward the end of the year. I made all of the programs. In the first 40 features, I was only out of the top four finishers twice. There were more manufactured chassis than ever. The one I was running was built by my boys and I, so every good finish meant a little more."

Ken Matthews and Bob Mackesy stood out in semi-feature action at Golden Sands in 1978. Orv Buelow, John Halverson, Gary Porter, Kirby Kurth and Les Stankowski stopped to take the honors when Matthews and Mackesy didn't.

Tom Reffner got things underway at Kaukauna by defeating Larry Detjens in the spring opener. Detjens' car lost most of its fine tuning in a collision with Evert DeWitt, but he still managed to hold off Reffner until lap 39. Dick Trickle won both the Red and White races. He got a little help from fate when Larry Schuler and Tom Reffner collided in the first event and Reffner was sidelined. In the second event, Trickle struggled with overheating problems to hold off Reffner and Marzofka. In the Blue race, Mike Miller took advantage of a blistered tire on Reffner's Concord to win.

Dick Trickle recovered from a slide along the wall in which he lost a dozen positions to win the ARTGO opener at Grundy. When ARTGO racing returned to Grundy in June, Tom Reffner got his first ARTGO win since 1975. He won one 50-lap feature and finished the other in a tie with Trickle. Trickle caught Reffner and then on the white flag lap took to the outside to edge ahead. Reffner got the edge back in turn four and it took a final burst of speed on Trickle's part to earn a tie. On Memorial Day, Dick Trickle was the overall winner in the ARTGO show at Capital Speedway in the first race. Trickle took the lead on lap 27 and left Bob Senneker, Joe Shear, Ed Hoffman and Larry Detjens fighting for second. In the second feature, Bob Senneker made some quick moves to get through traffic on lap 22. Trickle finally got through but couldn't make up the quarter-lap lead Senneker had built up. Rusty Wallace dominated the next ARTGO show at Capital, and then Tom Reffner won the Pepsi Monza race there. It gave him enough points for the overall championship for the second year in a row.

It was a year when central Wisconsin drivers traveled far and wide in search of victory. Dick Trickle won the April Foolin' 100 at Westchester, Ohio. Rodney Combs led the race for 55 laps before a piece of metal off another car went through his radiator and sidelined

Steve Burgess

him. Trickle took the lead and never relinquished it. Then Trickle traveled to Hartford, Michigan to win an ASA 100-lap race. He passed Rusty Wallace to capture a 100-lap event at Springfield, Missouri, then closed out the season by winning the National 200 at Rockford and the World Cup 400 at Odessa. In the race at I-70, Mike Eddy, who had led 320 laps, slipped coming out of turn four on lap 386, and that was all Trickle needed to get by him.

Tom Reffner won the 100-lap Missouri Championship race at Springfield in July. In September, he traveled to Elko to win a Superamerica 100-lap feature and then in the twilight of the season, he again went to Colorado Springs and won the 150-lap race held there.

Larry Detjens celebrated one of many great days in his career when he put down all contenders at the Minnesota Fair.

JOHNNY ZIEGLER

Crawling into a bear's den

O ne of Johnny Ziegler's loves is bow and arrow hunting and on one occasion he was hunting bear out west. A bear was spotted and the dogs took off in pursuit. Finally the bear ran into a den. The dogs chased the bear right into the den and as the growling and howling was going on inside the earth, Johnny and the guide discussed what should be done. "You just crawl in the opening and shoot the bear," the guide instructed Johnny. "The dogs will keep the bear occupied. You don't have to worry unless the dogs decide to leave the den." Johnny thought about it, got down on his hands and knees, and worked his way through the open-

Johnny Ziegler

ing of the den to the spot where the bear and dogs were having at it. He shot the bear. The story says a lot about Johnny Ziegler's courage. It also goes a long way in illustrating why he was one of the top short track drivers in Wisconsin.

Johnny Ziegler got out of drag racing because he considered the 60-mile tow to Union Grove too far. Now he travels much further as one of the Midwest's finest drivers. His first stock car was a Studebaker that the owner of a salvage yard was generous enough to give

145

him. When he went to a paint store and asked for some free paint, the owner of the store gave him a can of Euclid green. It has been Johnny's color ever since. Johnny Z destroyed the hobby stock car in five races. In 1968 he built a 1959 Ford and won three out of the first four races he was in. That prompted a switch to late models. At the same time that Johnny was beginning his racing career he was also beginning married life. "Long before I met Johnny," Sandy Ziegler recalls, "my parents used to go to Jefferson Speedway. The ticket takers collected the money at the gate as you drove in. We were poor and in order to save money, my friend Carol and I would get in the trunk. One night she leaned on a can of bug spray and I thought we would die.

"I met Johnny at the midget races in Sun Prairie. I was 16 and it was the first time I was there. I overheard him say, 'Those girls look like they are here to get picked up.' I showed him my parents car keys and told him I drove to the races. Later, at school, a girl came up and said he wanted to go out with me. I said, 'No, he is ugly.' At that time there was a place on the square in Madison where 13- to 18-year-olds could go and dance. During a break in the music, I went down to an ice cream shop to get a tin roof sundae. He stopped me and asked if I wanted a ride home. I told him my parents were picking me up. Two weeks later I went out on a date with him to the midget races and I never went out with anyone else after that."

Sandy has been his constant companion at the races, but would be missing on the night he won his first late model feature at Columbus. By race time the car had a blown head gasket and Johnny didn't think he had a chance of winning. His wife, Sandy, was sick so he told her to go home. He would run a couple of laps and load up and come home. The race was filled with wrecks and Ziegler avoided them all and won the race. The Columbus track continued to be a favorite and Ziegler has won the track championship there six times.

Ziegler is a native of Madison and another track that he frequented early in his career was Capital Speedway in Oregon. He won four championships at the track. He also had some of his greatest crashes there.

One of those accidents occurred in 1974. Ziegler was driving a Mustang convertible with a powerful 474 cubic inch engine that sent the car rocketing down the straightaways. All Ziegler remembers is getting on the gas as he was trying to pass someone on the outside coming out of turn two. He looked and the right wheel was about 10 feet above the car. He never had a chance to take his foot off the gas pedal before hitting the wall.

Johnny Z smiles as he recalls another wreck at Capital. "I was set up to pass Al Moldenhauer on the inside when the throttle stuck. I went shooting toward the wall in turn one. Fortunately for me, Al was between me and the wall. It was like hitting a big sponge. I sliced his car about in half. After the dust and dirt settled, I looked over at Al and laughed. There he was, sitting with his goggles going straight up and down on his face. They were twisted in his helmet straps and he was struggling without luck to get them back in place."

"I worry more about Johnny getting injured doing other things." his wife, Sandy, claims. "One night he came home from playing hockey and said, 'I think I broke my neck.' He grabbed a six pack and we were off

Bobby Gunn and Minnesota star Mel Walen square off at Wisconsin Dells.

Whatever Fred Bender said, it must have been good.
to the emergency ward. He had a dislocated shoulder
and broken collarbone.

"The next year he came home after being hit in the
face with a puck. Seven teeth were missing. He was in
the dentist's chair eight-and-a-half hours the first day,
four the next, and four the next. He had to have 50
stitches, seven root canals and a cap. And what did he
say when it was all over? 'I was waiting for the dentist
to oil the drill.'"

Using Capital Speedway and Columbus as a home
base, Johnny and his crew began to race further and
further from home — Jefferson, Wisconsin Dells,
Kaukauna, LaCrosse and Rockford.

A 1972 trip to Rockford is an indication of how, at
that time, drivers visiting from other areas were treated.
Johnny and Ed Hume decided to take a pair of Mus-
tangs and test the talents of their neighbors to the
south. "They weren't competitive and they didn't want
a couple of hot shots coming down there and stealing
the show. Ed was leading and I was sitting back waiting
to race, when someone who was always wild down there
pulled up beside Ed and they crashed. Afterwards, in
the pits, someone took an axe to the roof of Ed's car.

"I won the race, but not without rubbing fenders, and as I was coming to a halt to pick up the trophy, a car smacked me in the rear. It was as if the driver wanted to say, 'You won, but I don't like it. Don't come back again.' I lost my temper. I could see him waiting at the end of the backstretch behind some cars that were stopped at the exit. I took a run down the back straight and did I hit him. I was so mad I was willing to sacrifice my whole car. The trouble was I hit him so hard I totaled the three cars in front of him. I tried to back up, but the engine killed. I still had my seat belts on so I was trapped when the drivers got to me. One driver reached in each window and grabbed one of my arms and stretched them out and another guy used my head for a punching bag. I really got it. I looked like a raccoon for a couple of days."

One of Johnny's greatest races occurred at Golden Sands in 1976. Tom Reffner was the main opponent in a 76-lap feature. "Tom Reffner was the man to beat at the time. I was leading when Tom came up on the outside of me and we ran side by side to the end. I won by about three inches. We may have rubbed some paint along the way, but as I recall there wasn't even a lot of that."

During 1976, Ziegler would also spend time racing against Michigan's finest drivers on Friday night at Hartford. Every Friday night he would race against Ed Howe, Tommy Meyer, Randy Sweet and Bob Senneker. Then they would drive all night and get home at 6 a.m. Ziegler would go to work and then travel to Wisconsin Dells to race against Dick Trickle, Tom Reffner and Marv Marzofka.

After the 1976 season, Johnny curtailed his racing activities and spent a great deal of time with his family and his businesses. He had been involved in a crane operation, but phased that out and moved into a landfill business. It absorbed all of his talents for a period of years.

After racing off and on in the sportsman and late model divisions, Johnny became more deeply involved in racing in 1981 when he and Charlie Yelk teamed up. They won the track championship at Capital Speedway and Slinger. "We had the Capital Speedway crown won by mid-season. In fact, we won so many features it was getting embarrassing. It was the first year of the 9:1 rule and Nickerson-Volden, our engine builders, just hit on the right combination. I remember the track official, Clem Droste, saying I would have to replace the spark plug holes because they had run so many compression tests. Dick Trickle was running a Ford small block and through no fault of his own they just couldn't keep it together. It was the worst season he ever had and it made things a lot easier for me. That Capital championship is one of my favorite memories."

From 1982 to 1984 Ziegler drove for Bob Ford. In 1985 he began to drive for Bob and Tom Reible of Watertown, Wisconsin. They had approached Ziegler in 1983, but had wanted to travel more than Ziegler was willing to do, so they then got Mark Martin to be their driver. Martin would drive for them for two years. When the driver's seat became open again in 1985, Johnny accepted the offer.

In 1986, driving for the Reibles, Ziegler won the overall Slinger Nationals title. It was a great accomplishment considering the talent that traditionally gathers for the event.

Johnny's favorite race for the Reibles may have been a 300-lap race that he lost at Capital Speedway in June 1986. "I looked up at the scoreboard on the 254th lap and realized everyone was running pretty hard and I wasn't. It was time to go. I caught up to Trickle, who was in first, and I think we got carried away. We ran 20 laps side-by-side and the crowd was going nuts. Dick was a huge favorite and I was the local boy."

Ziegler would take the lead, but later be penalized for running over a jack in the pits and dropped from contention. Later he joked with his wife, Sandy, "I thought from the thump I had run over Jared (their son). I knew if I had you would have killed me."

1979
Season of records

Dick Trickle and Tom Reffner were the rivals as the 1979 season got underway at LaCrosse. In the first race, they bumped while fighting for the lead and Mike Miller took advantage of their miscue, going on to win. In the second evening, Trickle took to the outside groove in his duel with Reffner. Reffner would work his way up on the inside, only to break loose and fade in turn four. Finally, on the last lap, Reffner inched ahead, only to be overpowered in the final stretch. Reffner won, and then Mark Martin won both ends of the Dr. Pepper twin 50's.

Greg Holzhausen had a brand new car demolished the first night out when he spun in the back stretch and came to a halt in the middle of the track. Dave Mueller of Marshfield slammed into him at full speed, knocking Greg unconscious and destroying his car. When racing resumed, Mike Miller took the checkered. Marzofka won, and then Trickle and Reffner got

Dick Trickle: "Winningest Short Track Driver in America."

into a classic duel, with Reffner getting the upper hand. Mike Miller watched Trickle inherit the lead when his own Cutlass was black-flagged. Reffner set a record, 20:033, in his 1978 AMX and then won the 50-lap race

151

on Bobby Allison Night. Rusty Wallace chased down Ted Musgrave, then Trickle got a sweep. Marzofka gave the lead to Miller and then took it back again to close out the month of July with a win.

Steve Burgess won the opening race in August, then Dick Trickle slammed the door on everyone. On Dave Marcis Night, Larry Detjens puffed an engine and took Marzofka and Burgess into the wall with him. Trickle was safely in front at the time. Trickle held off Miller twice and then arrived late but scored still another victory to close out the month.

Mark Martin came back for the Oktoberfest to set a new record of 19:587, and then Butch Miller won the first 100-lapper and finished third in the second for the overall championship.

The racers moved to Wausau on Thursday nights, where Mike Miller beat Tom Reffner by a fender length on opening night. Marzofka, Trickle and Detjens followed the leaders across the line. The second night out, Detjens lost a six-lap fender-to-fender duel with Miller. Miller remained tough the third night of action, warding off the best efforts of Tom Reffner in taking the feature. Reffner had his revenge on the next meeting, as he left Miller and Detjens fighting for second place.

Dick Trickle closed out the month of June by setting a record of 14:092 and then besting Marzofka's and Back's 1979 Camaros.

Mike Miller recorded his fourth feature victory at Wausau over the Fourth of July weekend. A week later, he split twin 30-lap features with Trickle. A quick replacement of a radiator by Miller's crew got him back into the second race, and he took the overall championship by one point.

August began with Trickle rolling a new 1979 Firebird off the truck and snapping up a checkered the first night out. The month ended with Miller and Trickle again sharing the honors in twin 30's.

Mark Martin showed up for Fan Appreciation Night in September and promptly set a record of 14:042. It

Bob Strait (88) and Jim Sauter (7).

Tom Reffner (88), the Blue Knight, takes the high side around Dick Trickle (99).

didn't last long because Dick Trickle revved up his Fire Chicken and came away with 14:040. In the 50-lap feature, it was Trickle over Martin by a fraction of a second.

Joe Krzykowski began the season as the strong man in the semi feature. Then Les Stankowski took over and, finally, Al Schultz put them all away.

The season at Capital Speedway started out as a good

one for Mike Miller. By the first week in June, he had
rung up four victories. Unfortunately, it was a bad year
for attendance at the speedway, and it closed its doors
on Friday night programs in mid-season.

Promoter Larry Wehrs decided to open with a bang
and got the season at Wisconsin Dells under way with
the Midwest Championships. Marv Marzofka used a second-place finish on Saturday night as well as first and
second-place finishes on Sunday to accumulate enough
points to win the overall championship.

In the first regular show, Mike Miller held off persistent challenges by Marzofka and Trickle on his way to
victory. The next week out, Miller took his "Ugliest Cutlass in America" for a Saturday night cruise after passing Steve Holzhausen.

June began with the Ridge Runner roaring through
the pack and working up beside Johnny Ziegler. They
tangled. Marzofka took the lead. Ziegler took to the infield grass. Tom Musgrave moved up to challenge
Marzofka but didn't have enough firepower to get
around him.

Tom Reffner halted Trickle's string of victories at two
in the Nabbefeldt Memorials. Marzofka set sail and was
gone on Bobby Allison Night. If Marvelous Marv had
good luck, Allison's was equally as bad. It began when
Bobby blew an engine in practice. Larry Wehrs adjusted
the schedule so that Allison would have more time to
change engines. After a great deal of work by his crew
and volunteer support from others, the engine was in
and he started in the back of the third heat. Hardly a
lap had gone by when the front runnner, Rocky "The
Flying Squirrel" Breezer, spun high and then slowly
rolled down toward the infield. Allison hit him head on
and the fan in his Concord collapsed against the radiator.

Again, Allison and his helpers went to work in the
infield, but time ran out and the effort was futile. Then
Mike Miller loaned him the Cutlass that had set fast time
for the evening. Polesitter Steve Holzhausen took an

early lead and then was passed by Doug Strasburg. A caution caused by oil from Johnny Ziegler's car bunched the field and Marzofka took advantage of it and got the lead. The fans then turned their attention to Allison, who had deftly been making his way through the field. The Flying Squirrel spun for the second time in the evening on lap 41 and Allison, who had worked his way up to sixth, moved past two more cars and then began to overtake Strasburg on the outside. For 11 laps, the two were side by side, and then they touched and spun into the infield in turn two. Dropped to the back, Allison worked his way back up to ninth before time ran out. After the race, Bobby climbed from the car, put his hand on Miller's chest, and asked, "How is your heart?" Then he laughed. "You didn't load it on the hauler with the wrecker did you?"

The next Saturday night at Wisconsin Dells, Johnny Ziegler dropped the record to 14:238, but at feature time it was Tom Reffner finishing ahead of Marzofka.

Tom Musgrave was all smiles on the first Saturday in July when he stepped to the pay booth and collected the lion's share of the purse. Trickle beat Marzofka and the field stayed as they started, while Breezer and Lund ran side by side with Breezer getting a last-lap victory.

Dick Trickle edged out Miller in his 1979 Firebird to begin August, but then Miller closed out the month with two victories.

It was a mad scramble in the semi-feature with Joe Krzykowski. Bob Lee, Don Turner, Dave Lalor, Jim Johnson, Steve Moll, Kirby Kurth and Greg Holzhausen all taking victories.

Trickle and Reffner were nose to nose in the opening races at Golden Sands. Reffner won. Trickle won. Then the two battled for the final two-thirds of a race. It ended with a desperate Trickle pushing the slower car he was trapped behind across the finish line. Larry Detjens ended a long winless streak before Reffner came back to score two more victories. Then Detjens came back and won the mid-season championship after Miller

Tom Reffner, center, and Dick Trickle, right, discuss racing strategy.

and Trickle bumped each other on lap 47. Detjens won again and then the season ended as it had begun with Trickle winning, but only after having battled Reffner right down to the wire.

Les Back made his father proud in the semi-feature. Joe Krzykowski. Gary Porter, John Brevick, Roy Bohm, Ted Musgrave and Bobby Turzinski were also not to be denied victories.

With the weather a touch above freezing on April 8, the specials got underway at Oregon, and Tom Reffner piloted his 1978 AMX to victory in the ARTGO opener.

After 26 starts, Dick Trickle found a dream coming true at Milwaukee when he took the checkered in the ASA Superamerica 150. Mike Miller hounded him to the finish and made Trickle's great moment in racing an honest effort. A sly move in the pits had Trickle changing three tires at once and gaining valuable time on every stop.

Dick Trickle won the spring opener at Kaukauna, and then the action returned to the ARTGO circuit, with Reffner and Senneker taking main events at Capital

Speedway. Mike Miller took the 100-lap ARTGO special at Lake Geneva after passing Reffner on lap 55. Reffner remained in pursuit but soon found himself trapped behind Tom Jones. On lap 63, they tangled and Jones found himself climbing a dirt bank and flipping. Tom Reffner won the ARTGO-LaCrosse NGK 200. The Grundy show went to Mike Miller. Then Trickle won five ARTGO features in 24 hours at Wisconsin Dells and Oregon, won the Dairyland 150 at Golden Sands and took home the ARTGO crown.

At Kaukauna, Trickle continued his winning ways in the Hi-Rev 100. He left the weekly point leader, Alan Kulwicki, fighting with Miller for second. Trickle took the "Red" race and then came back to edge Kulwicki in the "White" race.

Reffner and Trickle won the preliminaries at the Minnesota Fair but couldn't defeat Mark Martin in the final 300 on Sunday.

Larry Detjens found the whole season worthwhile when he went to Bakersfield, California in October and won $9,500.

RICHIE BICKLE, JR.
A father and son

Richie Bickle, Jr., grew up watching his father challenge the best in the Midwest. He knew he wanted to be a race driver before he ever graduated from high school. "I remember my dad racing against the Illinois drivers at Elko, Minnesota," Richie recalls. "He had to go three wide at times, but he passed everyone from his 19th starting position. No one could believe it."

When it was time to go racing on his own in 1977 he went down behind the barn and selected a 1968 GTO as his first race car. "It was so beat up you could hardly tell what it was," he says. "I put a battery in it and went racing. I led the first six laps and a driver got loose underneath me and T-boned me. I went off the track on the back stretch. The wreck destroyed the radiator, transmission, battery, and broke the roll cage. I couldn't believe I got hit that hard. It was probably the hardest I've been hit in my career."

Bickle then turned to a 1974 Pontiac which he raced in the sportsman class at Jefferson for the last half of the 1977 season and the 1978 season. At the time he raced at Jefferson on Saturday night and then raced motorcycles on Sunday. He stopped racing motorcycles in 1979, the year he graduated from high school.

"Racing at Jefferson was always exciting. There were six heats and I was always in the fourth heat. A lot of times it was three wide racing. One night a car came off the wall and I got pushed into the sand. It bent the stub over three inches. Instead of being slower, the car was faster and I won the semi-feature.

"One night I decided I was going to race at Capital Speedway, but my dad thought I was too young to know what I was doing on a half-mile track so he tore all the ignition out of the car. There was no way I was going to Capital and he knew I couldn't go without an ignition system."

In 1979 Richie Bickle, Jr., built a 1972 Ford Torino with a 302 cubic inch motor and started campaigning at mid-season. The first night out at Columbus he won his heat race and the semi-feature. The car also ran well at Lake Geneva and Rockford.

During the winter, he decided to cut the rear clip off and turn it into a Rockford car. Then he changed his mind, gave the old car away and built a new Rockford car. His circuit expanded the following summer to include Rockford, Lake Geneva and Capital Speedway, where he ran with the late models. He won 23 semi-features, more than anyone else in the United States, and was named the rookie of the year at both Rockford and Lake Geneva.

It was during the summer of 1980 that Richie found his first sponsor while racing at Rockford. On this particular evening Bickle started on the second row and was soon challenging the leader. While the leader had more power on the straights, Bickle finally passed him in a curve and held him off for the rest of the race, winning the semi-feature. After the race, Gene Ructi of Blackhawk Fire Protection approached Bickle and asked him what would make him faster. When Richie responded new headers, Ructi asked how much they cost. The answer was $75. Ructi paid for them and continued to sponsor Bickle for three years.

For the 1981 season Bickle turned his Rockford car into a late model and campaigned heavily at Lake Geneva where he finished in the top five in points. He finished ninth at Capital and also ran at Slinger and in some ARTGO races. "What I remember most about that season was that the night I won my first late model feature at Lake Geneva was the night Larry Detjens got killed at Kaukauna. My dad broke the news the next morning. You don't forget things like that."

That first late model feature win was important. "It was a learning year. The year before I ran a lot of semi-features and did well, but I was tickled to win that first late model feature. It made up for anything that was missing."

In 1981 Richie had improved his chances with a better motor. Intent on continuing to improve, he went to the bank before the 1982 season and borrowed $5,000 to buy a frame and cage. After the loan was approved he went to Rander-Car and bought as much as he could. He made plans to buy tires from Joe Shear. When the season started, he headed off for every track within 300 miles and ran every race he could. When the season was over, he had run between 90 and 100 races. He won a couple of local features and set fast time at the Dells. If the summer before found him in ninth, tenth or eleventh consistently, this summer found him running fourth, fifth and sixth at the end of the feature. At Slinger's banquet at the end of the year, he told the track owner, Wayne Erickson, that he was going to be their track champion in 1983. It was a promise Bickle would fulfill.

In 1983, Richie cut down on the number of races he was in and turned his attention to winning the track championship at Slinger. He would finish in the top five in 17 out of the 18 programs that were run at the track. The only time he didn't finish well, he broke a lifter in the hot laps. As a result he started dead last in the feature. He made his way through traffic and was passing Shear for second when he again experienced motor problems. The season was one in which both he and Joe Shear won about six features apiece, leaving little for anyone else.

But if his luck was good at Slinger, it was also a summer of blown engines. "I didn't crash," he says, "but when I blew an engine the car lifted off the ground." By the end of the year he had paid the bank back, but was broke. "I wasn't going to owe anyone anything so I went the cheapest way I could. I borrowed $1,500 from a pit crew member and bought a motor from Connie Bamburger and finished out the season with it."

Starting 1984 on a tight budget Bickle kept his old car, but still managed to buy a second Howe car. He decided to run Slinger, Kaukauna and Capital. Then, as the season progressed, Steve Marler became his sponsor. On the night that Bickle would first race with his new sponsor's name on the car, Marler Insurance Night at Kaukauna, he won the feature. While he ran well at Capital Speedway, his home track, his first feature win on a half-mile track would be at Kaukauna. Looking forward to the future, he continued to gain experience in the summer of 1984 by running primarily at Kaukauna, Slinger and Capital.

Patch Press Products became a sponsor in 1985 and it enabled Bickle to update his car, hauler and equipment. After getting the car to handle well, Bickle added a Carl Wegner engine and that gave his car some new found power. Richie won the season opener at Capital Speedway and then went on to win several more races at the track. Those wins and other good finishes enabled him to win the point championship at the speedway. The high point of the season at Capital Speedway came during the October Nationals. "I beat Joe Shear. It was the best dog fight race I've ever been in. He was right on my bumper. If I had slipped the least little bit, he would have passed me. It was neat. Everything went perfect for me at Capital that year." Bickle also had a good season at Kaukauna and in the ARTGO races that he ran. Richie Bickle felt it was a step up in his career. He had proven himself.

A Left-Hander Chassis and Wegner engines were at the heart of Richie Bickle's race efforts in 1986. Before the season was over, he had won 17 features and the points championship at Capital Speedway. He ran well at Slinger, Kaukauna and the Dells. At Slinger he captured the Coors 75-lapper. He closed the season by winning the Oktoberfest 200 at LaCrosse. "For the first time," he would comment, "I felt that wherever we went we had a chance of winning."

Richie started out the 1987 season with Miller sponsorship, with the goal of running well wherever he went. Once again he continued to extend his experience. In July, he tested the banks of Bristol. "After my first hot lap session I came in and the crew asked if the car was loose or pushing. I really didn't know. I was so caught up in it all. Wow! We qualified rotten, but I knew we would cook in the race. As the race wore on I was behind the leader, Dick Trickle, and I knew I had a stronger motor. I was just waiting for the last 25 laps before passing him. Before the race the crew had asked if I wanted a head strap and I told them no. My neck just went." Bickle finished second to Trickle. Again, it was a learning experience.

The 1987 season also gave Bickle the opportunity to win the biggest purse of his career, $15,000 at Calgary, Alberta. Butch Miller, who led most of the race, pulled in for a normal pit stop 60 laps from the end. The pit stop allowed Bickle and Ted Musgrave to pull into the lead. Miller returned to the track, but the race was red flagged because of rain and hail on lap 454.

Richie's radio was out and he didn't know he had won until after the race. "He couldn't speak," said a crewman. "If you blew on him it would have tipped him over."

"It was good to hit on something," said Richie, "after a year of flat tires. There aren't too many races with a purse like that. It was pretty neat."

Like many of his fellow racers on the Wisconsin circuit, Richie has moved on to NASCAR fame.

1980
Movin' on

When the lights were turned on at Wausau's State Park Speedway in 1980, it would be defending track champion Mike Miller who would return to narrowly defeat Marv Marzofka. The next week, Miller returned to set a track record of 14:114 and pass Dick Trickle in the final lap to take another victory. Miller scored a third victory, then Dick Trickle got by Miller on the 20th lap to snap Miller's string at three. May closed with Steve Moll recording his first feature victory, as he led from start to finish.

Marv Marzofka found things falling his way in early June when he took the lead on lap nine and then withstood two stiff challenges by Trickle. In the same month, Les Back found himself out front until Tom Reffner caught him on lap 14. Reffner went on to beat Larry Detjens by two car lengths. Earlier in the evening, Jim Dumdey spun and then was hit by Ron Waite, who ended up parked on top of Dumdey's car.

Dick Trickle might have caught Mike Miller, whose new Camaro was overheating, but he mistakenly thought he had a tire going flat and finished a cautious second. Mike Miller passed Steve Moll and again defeated Trickle, then Trickle came back and ran away from Marzofka, Reffner and Miller. The season ended with Miller once again being track champion.

Old names dominated the Wausau semi-features: Kirby Kurth, Les Stankowski, Roy Bohm, Orv Buelow, Rick Haase and Jimmy Back.

Opening night at LaCrosse was a repeat of opening

night at Wausau. Miller and Marzofka ran side by side until Miller got the upper hand on lap 15 and raced to victory.

Ralph Bakewell led the next Wednesday until he spun out. When the green fell with five laps remaining, Trickle found Mike Miller glued to his side but unable to pass him. Jay Sauter, up from the hobby ranks, began to show his talents by taking third. The next week, it was Miller who found Trickle right at his side but unable to get around him for ten laps.

Mark Martin won the overall championship in the Dr. Pepper special. In the first 50-lapper, he settled for second behind Trickle. He won the second race while in his rearview mirror, Joe Shear did the incredible in passing both Trickle and Miller on the last lap to finish second.

It was a June night and Bobby Allison, in town on other business, decided to

A championship trophy won by Marv Marzofka at LaCrosse.

drop by and watch the action. It didn't take long before he was behind the wheel of Mike Miller's car. Trickle and Allison dueled side by side until Joe Krzykowski blew an engine, bringing out a yellow. The green came out. Trickle and Allison exchanged grooves and were back at it until the finish, where Trickle won by a breath. Or did he?

Jimmy Back and Jay Sauter got together at LaCrosse and ended up against the wall. Reffner swept by the bunched pack on the restart and led Marzofka across the start-finish line. In the next feature, Dewey Gustafson, as he would often do, jumped off to an early lead. Ralph Bakewell caught him, then Mike Miller caught both of them and went on to hold off Marzofka and win the 40-lap event. Marzofka found himself in second again the next night of racing when he had enough power to get ahead of Trickle on the back stretch but couldn't stay with him on the front straight. Trickle got a sweep and then came back to win a feature that was delayed when Jay Sauter, Jim Back and Ralph Bakewell all ended up in the wall.

Marv Marzofka shook the losing-by-inches role on the first Thursday evening in August when he passed Steve Holzhausen and took the checkered. Mike Miller edged out Trickle on the last lap of the 50-lap Dave Marcis Special. LaVerne Grandall, running the best he ever had in a new Camaro, tangled with Don Turner in turn three to spoil the car's debut. The regular season ended with Marzofka being bridesmaid to Trickle twice. Mark Martin won the Oktoberfest race.

Les Back, sharing a car with his brother, Gary, still managed to dominate the semi-features at LaCrosse. If he wasn't there when the checkered dropped, LaVerne Grandall, Fred Beckler, Greg Holzhausen, Don Turner or Morie Delmore were.

Steve Moll carried the checkered at Wisconsin Dells when he took the lead on lap 15 and beat a hard-charging Marzofka to the finish line. Dick Trickle won the Nabbefeldt Memorial championship by finishing second to Joe Shear and then winning the final 50-lap event of the evening. Mike Miller kept Trickle behind him the next night, then Gary Back took to the track to beat his own father on Father's Day. Marzofka gave everyone a thrashing and then Mike Miller came back to finish ahead of Tom Reffner. Trickle and Steve Holzhausen both won, then Mike Miller had everyone watching, as he drove his new Camaro to victory. Marzofka edged Reffner, then Larry Detjens captured the 75-lap finale.

Mike Miller again found opening nights to his liking

when he finished ahead of Trickle and Reffner at Golden Sands on the first Sunday evening of racing. The second night out, Tom Reffner got by Marzofka on lap 20 and then held off Mike Miller. Miller celebrated Memorial Day weekend with a close victory over Larry Detjens.

Tom Reffner couldn't close the gap, and as a result, Dick Trickle won the first race in June. Marzofka finished second to Miller, then Reffner found himself unable to close the gap on Trickle. Reffner held off Miller. Then Trickle lost Miller in slower traffic. On July 27, in what would be the final race for late models at Golden Sands, Kevin Stepan beat Joe Krzykowski. Earlier in the evening, Ralph Jacobsen stood before a circle of drivers in the pit area and announced that the road runners would be taking over for the remainder of the season. Racing, in the immediate future, was over in the backyard of the men who made it famous.

Larry Detjens got ARTGO action going by taking the spring classic at Rockford but not without a stiff challenge from Joe Shear. Dick Trickle captured the ARTGO Midwest Championships at Wisconsin Dells, then everyone traveled to Illiana Speedway to do battle in the fog. Ed Hoffman and Dick Trickle shared checkers. Trickle won the ARTGO 100 at Lake Geneva, destroyed his car at Berlin, then jumped in a new one to take the overall ARTGO championship at Wausau. Larry Detjens won the 1980 Slinger Nationals, but only after Trickle claimed a new world record, 11:658, on the quarter-mile in time trials. Darrell Waltrip used Mark Martin's car to win the ARTGO NGK 200 at LaCrosse, and then it was Trickle again in the ARTGO All Star 100 at Rockford. The season came to an end with Mark Martin taking both 75-lap events at Capital Speedway.

Mark Martin passed Dick Trickle on lap 137 and took the Superamerica 150 at Milwaukee. Martin would return to Milwaukee in August to beat Trickle by a car length.

At Kaukauna, it was Trickle and Martin who again

Don Collins (4) noses up on Arnie Christen (17).

Dewey Gustafson (88)

shared the spotlight. In the first 50-lap event, Martin spent 17 laps door-handle-to-door-handle with Trickle but couldn't get by him. In the second race, Martin got through traffic early and raced off and hid. Joe Shear won the "Red" race and then repeated his trip to victory lane in the "White" and "Blue" races.

Shear found the going much more difficult in the National Championships at Rockford. He passed Jim Sauter on lap 137, but Sauter got him back as they went through traffic on lap 159. From that point on, Shear could do no better than move up beside Sauter.

1981
Dark summer

Capital Speedway again had the honor of breaking winter's spell when it opened on the last Sunday in April. Larry Detjens, driving a new white Packerland Packing Camaro, gave notice that he was going to be a dominant force during the season by running away from the field and leaving Johnny Ziegler, Jimmy Pierson and Fred Bender fighting for second. Detjens had some success, but at a tragic price.

The Dr. Pepper Special at LaCrosse belonged to Detjens, as he took both 50-lap features. In the first event, he took the lead from Mike Miller on lap 24 and then watched a challenging Dick Trickle fade in the mirror with a blown engine. In the second feature, Miller was again the victim, as Detjens took the lead for good on lap nine. The task of winning was made much easier when Miller and Tom Reffner were forced to drop out with blown engines at the halfway point.

Dick Trickle and Alan Kulwicki dominated the Slinger Nationals, with each taking a 75-lap feature in the first program and Kulwicki coming back to take the 200-lap finale. Rich Somers triggered a nine-car pileup the first evening when he drifted high, and Richie Bickle, Jr. swerved to avoid him and blocked the track. Larry Detjens and Joe Shear collided and then Bob Bennett crashed into the back of Detjens and flipped on top of the disabled Packerland Special.

On Wednesday night, fans gathered at LaCrosse. Marv Marzofka began his march toward another track championship by edging out Detjens and Trickle in the opener. The next night out, Larry Detjens held off Dick

One of the most successful racing seasons for Larry Detjens (25) culminated in a crash that took his life.

Trickle in the closing laps to claim the victory.

Dick Trickle won his fifth Red, White and Blue title at Kaukauna. Larry Detjens looked like a sure winner in the first race until a rear wheel snapped off his racer and he hit the back stretch wall at full speed, destroying the front of his racer. Dick Trickle inherited the lead and the victory. Joe Shear broke away after a 40-lap struggle with Jim Sauter, Dick Trickle and Alan Kulwicki to win the second race of the series. Al Schill brought the crowd to its feet when he destroyed his racer in turn four after blowing a tire. In the final race, Rich Somers and Johnny Ziegler were early leaders, but in the end, Trickle collected the honors.

ARTGO began its Wisconsin season at Wisconsin Dells and Larry Detjens took home the bulk of the purse by winning both 50-lap features. Mark Martin was the overall point champion in a Memorial Day show at Kaukauna, even though he finished behind the winners of the two 50-lap features, Larry Schuler and Jim Sauter.

Jimmy Back had to contend with a large yellow 91 in his mirror during most of the opener at Wisconsin Dells Speedway, but fought Marzofka off at the checkered. The next Saturday, Marzofka timed in fastest and came from the back of the pack to win the feature. Roy Bohm won the semi-feature, but only after a struggle with Don Turner. Larry Detjens and Mike Miller each won one of the Lyle Nabbefeldt Memorial 55's.

Larry Detjens took two of the first four features at Capital Speedway and then returned on Memorial Day to take two 50-lap features, ARTGO victories four and five. In the first, he broke away from Jim Pierson, Jim Sauter, Dick Trickle and Mark Martin, chased down Joe Shear by lap 37, and sailed on to victory. In the second event, Detjens rode on Shear's bumper until lap 48 when he passed Shear in turn three. Detjens returned on the next Friday night to take victory away from Johnny Ziegler.

The stars returned to Kaukauna on August 1, and while Junior Hanley and Jim Sauter won the feature events, it was before a hushed crowd. Larry Detjens, while racing with Alan Kulwicki, slid out of control on the back stretch infield grass for several hundred yards and then hit a guard rail at full speed. The guard rail buckled and caught the right side of Larry's spinning vehicle. Wisconsin lost one of its most brilliant and likable drivers. Two months later, sadness would again overcome the Midwest racing world when Watertown's Pat Schauer lost his life after his car crashed at full speed into the pit wall at Winchester, Indiana.

At Wausau, Marzofka and Reffner each won again before the final showdown between Marzofka and Trickle for the point championship on September 3. Marzofka won the first 30-lap feature, and the pressure was on Trickle, who finished third and knew that he had to win the final feature and that Marv could finish no better than third if the title was to be his. When the final feature was over, Trickle had won and Marv, who got caught in traffic, had to settle for a sixth-place finish. The two would go on to share victories in the postseason Larry Detjens Memorial race.

The warm smile and firm handshake of Larry Detjens was missed on the central circuit. The sound of his carefully prepared hemi engines and the colors of those meticulously painted cars never faded from memory. He was a man of many thoughts who explained the tough years in this way: "If you just ran fast, you would never learn. You learn from testing and struggling. Those years don't pay any bills, but they build character." Detjens was always a competitor: "Whether it is skiing or racing, I enjoy the competition. It is the greatest feeling on earth to be out on that track side by side with someone testing every nerve and skill in your body."

THE LADY IN BLACK

Turn left only

Ask Dick Trickle about driving at Daytona. Ask Jim Sauter about Talladega. Each track has its own characteristics. Richard Petty smiles as he tells his son, Kyle, about the hump at Charlotte and how to negotiate it. Darlington has long been known as "The Lady in Black."

The short tracks of central Wisconsin were no different. Each had its own secrets. Each presented its own challenge.

Wausau was Wisconsin's "Lady in Black." The race car had to be set up so the tires couldn't be spun. Spin them twice, and the show was over. The car was always loose. Drivers corrected for bumps before they got to them, knowing where they were. The inside groove was the fast one. The last of the quarter-miles, it had a unique personality. Veteran Don Ruder claims the track acquired its meanness from being built all wrong.

The front wall at Wausau proved itself fatal. Its sandbanks on the turns and back straight have torn frames from cars and launched others into oblivion. Beyond those sandbanks was a marshy pond that received Marlin Walbeck, "Snoozer" Wisnewski and Bobby Allison. While packed stands urged their heroes on to victory, they could become stacked up in turn one in an instant, leaving Jimmy Back wondering if he and his cohorts truly are professionals.

On the opposite end of the spectrum was Wisconsin Dells' third-mile, which had a reputation of "being what a short track should be." As a result, according to Dick Trickle, it was driven in a classic fashion. "You drop low in the corners and then drift high on the straights. You try to make the track into the roundest oval possible." Howard Johnson, one of the original owners, delighted in calling it the "Home of the Biggies." Ed Howe, The Green Hornet, and Tom Meier began a procession of name drivers brought in to compete against local talent. Homer Spink once drove his race car to the track with police in pursuit. Dick Trickle would probably have reenacted the scene if he were ever in danger of missing the Lyle Nabbefeldt Memorial Race, which he considered the most important race he ran all year.

At Wausau, the water hazards were off the track. For years, at Capital Super Speedway, the water hazards were created by springs that pushed water through the track on the back straight.

Bobby Weiss (38)

Steve Burgess (12)

Grubba

Capital's walls also demanded respect. Johnny Rank, Jim Sauter, Whitey Harris and Dick Trickle have tested them. "It seems like every time I go there, I put the fenders in the truck, the hood in the truck, and then I load the rest of the car," said Marv Marzofka after a collision with T.K. Shear put him head first into the front wall and left everything falling about in slow motion.

Tony Strupp tried scaling the wall and pit fence in turn two. Johnny Ziegler tested the concrete in turn two, "All I remember was that I was passing somebody on the outside. I looked, and the right front wheel was about ten feet above the car. The accelerator stuck, and I hit the wall going wide open."

The strategy at Capital? According to one veteran, you went into the corners way over your head, fully conscious that you are doing so. Then you stood on the brakes. The more you frightened yourself in doing so, the faster the lap you turned.

The deer along Highway 137 must have wondered where everyone was going so fast on Wednesday nights. The answer was LaCrosse Interstate Speedway.

"Sooner or later," said Tom Reffner, "you learn to respect the walls at LaCrosse." High speeds created bone-jarring wrecks and the brick-like composition seems to pull the car into it upon contact. Tom Reffner knows because he hit it hard enough to knock the fuel cell out of his car. Greg Holzhausen lost a brand new car there. Veteran drivers all have tales of respect.

"Some time pay close attention as the cars enter turn three," said Marv Marzofka, as he described another of the track's distinct characteristics. "Notice how they bounce around? It gets rather hairy."

Tom Reffner tells of a certain groove in turns three and four that worked for you if you caught it and "if you didn't plan on backing off." Most passing, unlike Wausau, was done on the high side. Momentum was such that the lower driver couldn't pull away.

Golden Sands' good quality was that spinning cars would drop off its high banks unharmed into the infield.

Inspection time at Capital Super Speedway.

If the track had a bad quality, it was that cars going over its edge got airborne. Some of the best drivers in the state have had that flight brought to an abrupt halt by the east retaining wall.

To run right at Golden Sands, drivers hung high on the straights for as long as they could and then dropped sharply into the turns. A new dimension was added to central Wisconsin racing by the fast timers who took the risk of driving in the third groove as a means of disposing of the slower drivers in front and getting a jump on the field.

No one went 200 miles an hour on a central Wisconsin short track, but the thrills were to equal anything experienced at Daytona or Talladega.

1982
The fast groove

LaCrosse Speedway opened its doors on April 28 and two veterans proved that they hadn't lost an ounce of talent over the winter. Marv Marzofka followed Dick Trickle around Jim Weber on lap 13 and the two were side by side down to the checkered. Marv would inch ahead on the back straight, and Dick gained it back on the front straight. Since victories are decided on the front straight, Dick collected the honors. Steve Carlson finished third, proving that the hobby division has produced some tough drivers; Tom Jensen brought the old Mike Miller Cutlass home fourth. Steve Holzhausen snapped up the semi-feature.

Trickle passed Weber again on lap four and sailed on to win on the next Wednesday evening. The third feature of the season found Steve Burgess taking an early lead from Steve Carlson. While Trickle was closing the gap, time ran out and Burgess took the title. Trickle overpowered the field the next night out, but Steve Burgess came back to be the overall Dr. Pepper champion. He won the first 50-lap feature after taking the lead from Jimmy Back and finished second to Tom Reffner in the second. Misfortune struck Trickle twice. An oil line clogged in the first race and the fuel overflow hose came off in the second, causing him to retire from both races. In the second feature, Jay Sauter spun and backed his Camaro into turn three. Jim Sauter spun at the same time, and later, Al Schill hit the wall in turn three.

Trickle recovered to take the next three features in

a row but not without stiff competition. He edged Jim Sauter after Burgess' chances of victory were wiped out by a flat tire. On the following Wednesday night, Sauter held off a furious charge by Burgess, while Tom Reffner and Marv Marzofka waited for an opportunity to challenge. The next time out, Sauter passed Tom Reffner on lap 11, only to have Reffner come charging by and duel him to the end.

Burgess then beat Trickle and, on the first night of racing in July, Jim Sauter edged Reffner and Trickle. Reffner had it hooked up at their next meeting and would not let Trickle by, as they dueled side by side through laps 13 to 16. Taking it to the limit, Trickle almost spun coming out of turn four but recovered to have at it again. The Blue Knight held him off, while Marzofka and Back finished third and fourth. July ended with Steve Carlson, followed by Tom Carlson, taking the checkered. In the closing lap, Trickle got around Joe Krzykowski and Steve Holzhausen for third.

Marzofka took an early lead, saw Trickle close it, and then held the White Knight off to win the first feature of August. The rest of the month belonged to Dick, as he won three features. His winning ways gave him the point championship. Marzofka, Reffner and Back, who won the last regular outing of the year, finished behind him.

When the haulers rolled down the road on Thursday night, the story wasn't going to be much different at Wausau. When the season was over, Dick Trickle had won the point championship. He started out strong by beating Tom Reffner and Jimmy Back to the checkered in the first two features to be run there. Mike Miller interrupted his march on the checkered by beating Marzofka and Trickle in a close dice for victory. It was Trickle again on June 3, and then, after a 20-lap battle with Reffner, Trickle took the Sunkist 50. While Trickle got the lead briefly on lap 27 the next time out, Tom Reffner was the eventual winner. Marv Marzofka and Kevin Stepan won the twin 25-lap features on Larry

Jimmy Back and Johnny Ziegler lead the pack into turn one at Capital Super Speedway.

Detjens' Memorial night, but again, Trickle finished high enough to be the overall point champion.

Tom Reffner pushed his car to the limit in a contest for victory the following Thursday night, while Trickle looked on from third. Then it was Trickle for two weeks in a row, giving him seven victories at State Park Speedway. Marv Marzofka passed Lyle Nowak on lap 17 and outdistanced the pack for a victory and then went on to trade victories with Trickle in the season finale.

At Capital Speedway in Oregon, Roy Shackleford got things started in a Bac-Kar by leading the first 19 laps in the feature. Then Joe Shear took over and led Jim Sauter and Johnny Ziegler to victory.

Bob Gunn edged out Willie Goeden on the second night of competition. Tom Reffner emerged as the overall ARTGO champion, as he and Mike Miller won 50-lap features on Memorial Day. Steve Burgess and Dave Watson finished one-two twice and then were beaten by Joe Shear. Jim Sauter took the honors, and then Joe Shear swept into command, winning seven features in a row. On July 23, he pulled away from Dick Trickle when four caution flags, caused by the spins of Jim Weber,

178

Fred Bender, Jerry Wood and Steve Burgess, closed the gap. On August 13, it was Shear over Trickle again, and then Trickle won the next time out when Shear withdrew for the evening before the trophy dash was run. On August 27, the crowd froze, but Jimmy Back was hot, as he narrowly beat Ted Musgrave to close out the season.

It was a Saturday night of destruction on opening night at Wisconsin Dells. Before the third lap had been run, Tom Jensen, Keith Nelson and Al Schill had mixed it up in turn three. Jensen returned to spin on the 19th lap, taking Morie Delmore, Jim Back and Jim Weber with him. Then Steve Burgess spun on lap 33, and later Jim Weber hit the wall. Young Kevin Stepan looked like a seasoned pro, as he winged his way through traffic and edged out Reffner and Marzofka in the 50-lapper.

Steve Burgess captured both 55-lap Lyle Nabbefeldt Memorial races. In the first, he roared past Tom Reffner, Jim Weber, Steve Holzhausen and Jim Sauter and on to victory. Marv Marzofka had built up an insurmountable lead in the second feature, only to have it wiped out when J.J. Smith blew an engine and bunched the pack under the yellow. Two laps into the restart and Burgess had passed Marzofka. Marzofka came back to beat Reffner by a car length the next Saturday night and then repeated his winning ways the next week, as he survived a seven-car, red-flag wreck to beat Bobby Gunn.

Gunn won the Holiday 50 on July 3, and then it was wrecker time again. Rocky Breezer and Ron Beyer got things going by tangling on the opening lap. On the seventh lap, a five-car wreck eliminated Marv Marzofka and Bobby Weiss. Bobby Gunn and Jim Back traded paint on the 19th lap. Rocky Breezer spun again on lap 22 before things settled down and Tom Reffner went on to win the 50-lap event.

Tom Jensen took the early lead the next weekend, but in the end it was Johnny Ziegler holding off Steve Moll. Jensen was not to be denied the next time out. The month of August belonged to Jim Back. He beat

Joe Shear to the line in the 71-lap Dave Marcis Night feature, won again the following Saturday, and then overcame Tom Reffner, who experienced brake problems, to take the 50-lap championship race. Dan Przyborowski and Steve Holzhausen sent people home with something to talk about for the winter and mechanics home with a lot of work to do when they began what would be a 10-car wreck.

Marv Marzofka turned two victories and consistent driving throughout the year into the final track championship of his career.

Golden Sands gave late model action one more try. On June 6, Marv Marzofka, Mike Miller and Dick Trickle swept the dust off the finish line as they roared under the flagman three wide. Officials declared Marzofka the winner. The following week, Tom Reffner held off the persistent Mike Miller. Then the oval fell silent again. Central Wisconsin racers starred elsewhere during the summer. Jim Sauter had things going his way at Kaukauna until a mid-summer collision with the front straight wall left him with a broken ankle. Johnny Ziegler ran with the leaders all summer at Slinger.

Dick Trickle was the class of the field, as Wisconsin opened the season of special events with the Badgerland 150 at Milwaukee. He had reeled in the front runners, Bob Senneker and Alan Kulwicki, by lap 120 and was setting sail for the checkered when vibrations

Steve Carlson (50) edges ahead of Rick Wateski (93).

caused him to slow on lap 129. Senneker went on to hold off Kulwicki for the victory.

Tom Reffner set the early pace in the first of the Red, White and Blue races, but when his engine failed, Dave Watson swept on by to pick up the victory. Joe Shear, Jim Sauter and Johnny Ziegler followed him across the line. Sauter came back to win the White race by passing Watson on lap 23. In the final race of the series, Steve Burgess led until lap 24, when Watson, running with a borrowed engine and transmission, overhauled him. Joe Shear passed Burgess on lap 31, and then Dick Trickle and Jim Sauter gave Burgess the high-low treatment on lap 33. Trickle

For Dick Trickle, the most prestigious race in Wisconsin was the Miller 200. He would not win it until 1982 and it would take a carefully prepared new car. "The bottom line was I needed to win this race more than any other," he said afterward.

and Shear caught Watson but faded in the final laps.

Alan Kulwicki massed enough points to emerge as the overall winner in the first segment of the Slinger Nationals by winning the first 75-lap feature and then finishing second to Dick Trickle in the nightcap. Jim Sauter brought the crowd to its feet by getting on his roof in turn four. In July, Trickle won both 100-lap segments of the evening's program to claim the summer's title.

In ARTGO Racing, Jim Sauter got by Joe Shear's faltering racer on the 91st lap of 150 at Kaukauna and then outmaneuvered Dave Watson in late traffic to win the race. Joe Shear was the star of the July 4 Capital Speedway twin 75's. The first race got off to a slow start when a six-car crash, in which Dick Trickle tore the right front off his car, brought out a yellow. On the very next lap run under green, a seven-car wreck eliminated Tom Reffner and Wayne Lensing. When the race resumed, Shear caught Mike Eddy and passed him for the victory. In the second feature, Jim Sauter started strong but faded with ignition problems. Steve Burgess passed him and then held off Joe Shear for the victory. At the end of August, Jim Sauter returned to Kaukauna without the cast he had received from an earlier accident there and won the ARTGO 100 but only after an 85-lap duel with Joe Shear. Shear and Sauter shared 50-lap victories at Capital's Summer Nationals. Jim Sauter went on to take his second ARTGO championship, with a mid-September victory at Wisconsin Dells.

The thrill of victory ran through Dick Trickle's veins as it never had before when he won the Miller 200 at State Fair Park. "It was the race I wanted to win more than any other," he said joyfully in victory circle, "because it has more prestige than any other in Wisconsin."

Jim Sauter returned to the victory circle at Kaukauna in early September when he outdrove Joe Shear, Dave Watson and Dick Trickle to take the 100-lap feature sponsored by Budweiser. Joe Shear captured his fourth National Short Track Championship at Rockford in late September. The season ended in October at LaCrosse with two of central Wisconsin's favorites being the stars of the annual Oktoberfest. Tom Reffner won one of the 100-lap features, and Jim Back was the overall champion as a result of finishing second and third in the two main events.

1983
The mountain goats
get tougher

The 1983 season would see Dick Trickle traveling out of state more than ever before. In his absence, Jim Back and Tom Reffner dominated central Wisconsin racing. When Trickle did race in Wisconsin, he continued to show why he was the winningest short-track racer in the United States. At LaCrosse, Trickle won with such consistency that the bounty was brought back. At Wausau, while he did not win as often, Trickle would be the points champion.

On the opening Wednesday night in LaCrosse, Jim Sauter and Dick Trickle sandwiched Jim Weber in between them on lap eight and roared into turn one full bore. Trickle would emerge the leader and go on to beat Sauter by two car lengths. It was the end of June before Trickle's name would drop from the headlines. He won three straight features in May. On May 4, he had a clean sweep and had brushed by Jim Weber on his way to victory in the feature by the eighth lap. Rick Wateski brought the wrecker flashing from the pits early in the race when he exchanged paint with Monte Gress coming down the front straight. As Wateski slid through turn one, he forced Tom Thurk into the wall and then had Mike Niles slam into the side of his disabled vehicle.

Quick repairs kept Trickle's string going on to May 11 when he made contact with the wall during the fast dash and moved the rear axle of his racer in a foot. Jim Bohmsach, Vic Getzloff and the crew worked frantically to have the car repaired by feature time. In the feature, the car ran as well as ever and Trickle moved through traffic to catch his last opponent by the 13th lap. At the finish it would be Trickle, Jim Sauter and Jim's son, Jay, rounding out the top three. Jim Sauter would be the victim on the last Wednesday in May when Trickle got by him on the 18th lap. The first three across the line would be Trickle, Jim Back and Tom Reffner.

On June 1, Trickle edged out Tom Reffner at the checkered flag in a race that saw Mike Chase, a Californian who had come to see how it was done, spin out and take with him Jay Sauter, Steve Holzhausen, Ken Christenson, Bob Weiss and Ed Holmes. That Sunday was the running of the traditional Dr. Pepper races, and Trickle took both 50-lap races. Joe Shear, Jim Sauter, Bob Iverson and Jim Back would follow him across the line in the first race. In the second race, Trickle limped across the line on a flat tire ahead of Jay Sauter, Joe Shear and Jim Sauter. The following Wednesday, Trickle got a clean sweep, passing Back for third, Rick Wateski for second, and then running down Jim Weber for first.

The LaCrosse businessmen put a $700 bounty on Trickle's head, but it went uncollected the first night, as Trickle was out of town. There was excitement, nonetheless, as Jim Back chased Jay Sauter for six laps and finally passed him on the inside going through turn one on the last lap of the feature. The next Wednesday night, before the largest weekday night crowd in history at LaCrosse, Trickle returned and lost the showdown to Steve Burgess.

In early July, LaCrosse Interstate hosted the area mid-season championships and Steve Holzhausen dominated the three-day event. Coming on strong behind him in the area event were Ken Christenson, Jr., Greg Holzhausen and Steve Carlson.

The rest of the month belonged to Trickle and Reffner. Trickle nailed Jay Sauter by a car length, while Reffner and Back were hopelessly snarled in traffic. He then returned to hunt down Bryan Reffner in turn one

Gary & Lester Back

Billy Oas

Mike De Mars

of the last lap. This time he collected his own bounty of $600. On both of the other July events, Tom Reffner proved to be too strong for Ted Musgrave in the final laps.

Jay Sauter, who had been flexing his young muscles all season long, got in the victory column on the first week in August. He took to the outside groove and dared anyone to pass him on the inside. It worked, as Steve Carlson moved up and tried for four laps before fading. Then Dick Trickle moved up and tried lap after lap. He pulled even but could never draw out in front.

In mid-month, Trickle passed Steve Carlson and Jim Sauter for a victory and then came back to beat Bryan and Tom Reffner across the line. Trickle was denied victory in still another event when he was disqualified for refusing to sell an engine claimed by Steve Holzhausen. Trickle had blown his Central Wisconsin Racing Circuit 9:1 engine, and when he tried to slip in a more expensive ASA Prototype engine, the observant Holzhausen took note and claimed it. Jimmy Back was declared the winner as a result.

August closed out with Ted Musgrave passing Steve Carlson on lap 17 and speeding on to his first victory at LaCrosse. In the only event of September, Tom Reffner shaded the eventual point champion, Dick Trickle, and the CWRA champion, Jim Back. In the Oktoberfest, Ted Musgrave lost it momentarily in turn one, but that was enough for Reffner to get by. Musgrave never regained the lead, but he did hold off Back for second.

No one dominated the semi-features at LaCrosse during 1983 and the list of winners was a long one — Ed Holmes, Bryan Reffner, Joe Krzykowski, Greg Holzhausen, Donnie Fowler, Jim Weber, Jim Johnson, Bob Stephen, Doug Poeschel, Royce Rossier and Tom Carlson.

While Dick Trickle would emerge as the Thursday night point champion at Wausau, he found victory circle much more elusive. The season opened with him getting the best of Back and Reffner, but then Reffner came back to out-sprint him in the last two laps of the 30-lap feature. Reffner was victorious again on the next Thursday when he passed Kevin Stepan on lap 17 and then held off a hard-charging Trickle. A determined Trickle came back, and on the next night of racing he drove 19 hard laps to edge Reffner at the flag.

Kevin Stepan got by Joe Krzykowski on lap 22 and then fought off the late challenges of Bobby Turzinski to win his first feature. Young talents used 1983 to offer serious challenges on the circuit. At LaCrosse, Jay Sauter made his presence felt. At Wausau, Lyle Nowak, who overcame the handicap of driving with one hand, began to be listed among the veterans. June 16 found him in the shadow of Tom Reffner's back bumper as they crossed the finish line. Nowak was strong enough to defeat Trickle and Back. Jimmy Back shaded another hometown youngster and strong competitor, Kevin Stepan, in the first of two mid-season championship races. Dick Trickle finished just ahead of Back in the second feature.

Jim Dumdey had it going his way early in the running of the Larry Detjens Memorial Race. Wayne Lodholz passed him on the seventh lap, and then Kevin Stepan took command on the 16th lap and did some fancy driving in the final laps, as Mike Miller applied the pressure. Ted Musgrave was third; Dick Trickle was fourth. Jim Back opened and closed the month of July with victories as he edged first Ted Musgrave and then Steve Holzhausen. Holzhausen opened the month with a bone-jarring flip and then came back to get revenge by beating Tom Reffner and Bob Mackesy to the flag. In the other feature event of the month, a 50-lap affair, Jim Dumdey led for 22 laps before surrendering the lead to Dick Trickle, who went on to outdistance Tom Reffner for the victory.

Ted Musgrave cleared traffic early, chased down Rick Haase and then maintained a huge gap between himself and Back, Nowak and Trickle to begin the month of August. Trickle came back with a victory, and the two Bac-Kars of Reffner and Back had fans holding their breath as they witnessed a duel in which Reffner eventually emerged as victor. Trickle and Reffner shared the victories on championship night, but Trickle ended up being the point champion for 1983. Ted Musgrave turned Rib Mountain back to the skiers after winning the finale.

In the semi-feature, Greg Holzhausen and Jim Dumdey each got three victories in the course of the summer. The rest of the checkered flags were shared by Wayne Lodholz, Les Stankowski, Sonny Immerfall, Bryan Reffner. Rick Haase and Joe Krzykowski.

"It had to be the dumbest thing we ever did," comments Tony Zidar about his, and his brother Bob's, decision to purchase Capital Super Speedway. "We had never promoted a race. We had never seen a race on an asphalt track. We couldn't even see what we were buying because it was covered with snow. Never buy a race track covered with snow."

When the snow melted, the Zidars found there were a lot of repairs to be made. Concrete was poured for 29 rows of grandstand seats and the concession stands and bathrooms were remodeled.

Another project was the building of a quarter-mile track inside the half-mile so that the Jefferson sportsman could add another facet to racing at the speedway. The successful addition to the program was dominated by Ron Bishofberger, Lyle Phillips, Al Buedler, Andy Wendt and Rick Nelson.

In the late model division, the action was tight. Conrad Morgan showed early potential that would lead to a track championship. Morgan slipped by Jimmy Back on the back straight to take the first feature of the year. Morgan was leading the second but collided with Ed Holmes in the late-going and ended up watching Bob Gunn win a duel with Steve Burgess. Johnny Ziegler closed out May by dominating the competition on the track, but losing the race in the pits, where frowning officials found his car underweight.

Pat Schauer (21) battles Jimmy Back (61) at Golden Sands.

Fluff Furo (33)

Jay Sauter (58) grabs the lead.

Jim Weber started June out with a bang by winning two features in one evening, shading Bob Gunn and Arnie Christen, but it was Ed Bobzien who provided the fireworks. Bobzien's car crashed against the wall on the front straight, and then, as Ed was crawling out, it burst into flames that defied firemen for over an hour.

Arnie Christen was rolling along toward victory as the laps counted down the next night, only to brush the wall and bring out a yellow. After the yellow, Steve Burgess held off a determined Jim Back for the checkered.

Conrad Morgan won the next two features but had to do some exceptional driving in the second, as Rich

Bickle, Jr. and Bobby Weiss traded paint coming out of turn two. As Bickle destroyed his car against the wall, Morgan spun out and then regained control in the infield and came roaring back on the track in pursuit of victory.

Bob Gunn, Jim Weber, Steve Burgess and Joe Shear were the headliners in July. Weber's victory came only after Jim Back brushed the back straight wall, and, as usual, Jimmy had an explanation. It wasn't he who hit the wall, it was the wall that moved in and got him.

Mark Martin nailed Tom Reffner and Jim Weber and dominated the early-going, but Joe Shear slowly reeled in all three, as the first feature of August unfolded. On August 12, before a crowd of 4,000, Tom Reffner was followed across the line by Ted Musgrave, Jim Back and Shear. The next week it was Shear, Reffner and Musgrave. Then, in the 40-lap season championship, Ted Musgrave proved to be too much for Tom Reffner and the trailing pack. It was Reffner in the final regular event of the year and the 83-lap Capital Nationals in October.

The Zidars staged a Super Series that found Joe Shear relentlessly tracking down Tom Reffner, Dick Trickle outrunning Jim Back, and Joe Shear returning to hold off Ted Musgrave, Reffner and Trickle.

Semi-feature winners at Capital made up a roster of their own: Jerry Eckhardt, Russ Gray, R.J. McLeod, Wayne Lensing, Dave Lalor, Rich Bickle, Jr. and Don Leach.

Fans gathered at Wisconsin Dells and watched Tom Reffner, Jim Back and Bob Gunn trade victories and battle for a point championship that Back eventually won. Tom Reffner started things out by outwitting Steve Holzhausen in the 50-lap opener. Rocky Breezer spun on lap 17 and then spun again on lap 18, as he, Morie Delmore, Rick Wateski and Ken Christenson, Jr. all found the track too narrow on the back straight. Bob Gunn, Jim Back and Jim Weber shared honors in the month of June, with Gunn and Weber winning the Nabbefeldt 55's.

Larry Wehrs didn't have to bring along any fireworks on the Fourth of July. There were 50 laps of sparks and smoke on the track. Steve Holzhausen was just backing off on the fifth lap in turn three when a water hose slipped off and sent him and two others spinning. After the water dried, Rich Lofy did a solo in to the infield on the front straight. On the restart, Mel Walen sent the photographers running, as he bounced along the guardrail on the front stretch. Rocky Breezer, Christenson, Holzhausen and Ted Musgrave gave starter Bill Gronley reasons to wave the yellow on lap 22. Gronley unfurled the yellow again on lap 30, and Breezer, Bob Turzinski and Christenson crashed on lap 32 for another three-car bash, and on lap 33 when Rick Smith tested the front wall. On the restart, Bob Gunn took the lead from Steve Carlson and went on to hold off Ted Musgrave and Steve Holzhausen for the win.

The gremlins remained at work the next night out. Tom Reffner won the feature, but Ron Beyer provided the sparks in the semi-feature when he lost control in turn four, had the car climb the wall and then slide to a rest on its roof in turn one. Tom Reffner and Jim Back each won two features before Bob Gunn returned in mid-August to hold Steve Holzhausen, Reffner and Back at bay. Back beat Reffner and Gunn by an eyelash. Dick Trickle made it look easy, and then Steve Holzhausen won the 50-lap championship race.

While Jim Back and Tom Reffner established themselves as the weekend favorites at home, Dick Trickle traveled. Trickle won the opening ARTGO show at Rockford. It was a race in which Jim Sauter had everyone holding their breath when he slid through the oil of Joe Shear's blown engine, smashed into the pit entrance wall and stood the car on its nose. Before Sauter's car could drop back to the track, it was hit by another car and sent airborne, parts flying everywhere. On July 16, Trickle got the jump on Joe Shear at the start of the race and went on to notch a record 11th ARTGO victory. On August 2, in an ARTGO 100 at Kaukauna, Trickle

191

The packed pit area at Capital Super Speedway.

passed Mark Martin on lap 64 and went on to collect his own $1,000 bounty.

Trickle won ASA victories in places as distant as Coeburn, Virginia and Cayuga, Ontario. It was at Cayuga that Trickle had a run-in with his chassis supplier, Junior Hanley. You don't bump a Canadian in Canada, and Trickle bumped Junior on the 186th lap of the 200-lap race to take the lead. "I guess I spun the boss, but I could get back on the throttle faster coming off the turns. Bob Senneker had been tapping me ... we'd all been tapping each other ... for lots of laps." That week Junior Hanley sent Trickle a one-sentence certified letter asking for his equipment back.

Trickle won the Red, White and Blue Series at Kaukauna and won the Slinger Nationals title by beating Jim Sauter, Mark Martin, Gary Balough, Joe Shear and Bobby Allison.

The racing season in the Midwest had been put to rest when 49-year-old Jim Back decided to celebrate his winning the Central Wisconsin Racing Association's Old Style Circuit Crown by taking a trip to Bakersfield, California. When he arrived, he found himself at a distinct disadvantage. Everyone had to weigh the same, but his western competitors were all using brute-sized engines compared to his 355. To his credit, Back made the field and finished 11th in one of the two 75-lap features. Then he was off through the mountains to Carson City, Nevada. As his van towed the trailer and race car up the steep inclines, all of the lower gears were lost. The van could not tow its load in high gear but Back was not to be undone. He backed the race car off the trailer and pushed the rig through the mountains. When the gears in the transmission of the van began to growl, Back knocked a hole in the floorboards and ran a funnel down to the transmission. Whenever the gears sounded off, another quart of fluid was quickly added. On and off the track, life for Jimmy Back kept rolling on.

AL SCHILL

From salvage yard to race track

Al Schill, owner of Al's Auto Salvage in Franklin, Wisconsin, is one of those rare race drivers equally at home on dirt or asphalt.

Al Schill

To prove it, he won track championships at his home track in Hales Corners, which is dirt, in 1973, 1977, 1978, and 1979. He also won championships on the dirt track at Cedarburg, Wisconsin, in 1977 and 1979. After competing seriously on the ARTGO circuit for a few years, Schill chose a Shaw car to renew his quest for still another championship at Hales Corners on Saturday nights.

Sunday nights found Schill switching mounts, this time to a Frings chassis, and heading for one of the fastest quarter-mile paved tracks in the world at Slinger, Wisconsin. He first became track champion there in 1984. The 1986 title was the most difficult in the string of titles as he, Lowell Bennett and Rich Somers all had a chance of claiming the crown on the final night of racing.

"I won the championship by winning the feature," says Schill. "I finished first and Lowell finished second. If it had been the other way around he would have won the title."

Schill's racing career began on dirt in his brother's car at Hales Corners when he was 16. At the time the track did not permit anyone to drive until they were 21. When no one was watching the switch was made. Others may not have known, but his mother, who had to stand outside the fence because women weren't allowed in the pits, was always aware of what was happening.

In 1966, Al officially got his career underway in a 1955 Chevrolet that he raced at Hales Corners and Milwaukee's State Fair Park. While his father would not let him race at the other two tracks that formed a circuit at the time — Slinger and Cedarburg — Al finished 13th in the points and was named rookie of the year.

In 1967, Schill made the move into the Southeastern Wisconsin modified circuit, which headlined some of the Milwaukee area's hottest drivers — Miles Milius, Don Schuppel, Willie Goeden and Fuzzy Fassbender. Dennis Frings built the chassis for him and it sported a 1967 Nova body, rather than the traditional Ford coupe metal. Weighing only 2,000 pounds, Schill could pick up the front end with the motor in it. Schill won the IRA (Interstate Racing Association) championship the first year out in the car.

In 1970 and 1971, he raced six nights a week beginning on Tuesday night at Beaver Dam. Then he went to Blue Island, Frances Creek, Rockford, Wilmot and Lake Geneva. At the time, the same car could be used on dirt and asphalt. All one needed to do was change tires, shock settings and make a few other minor adjustments. A 6.66 Ford rear end was standard for all tracks except half miles.

It was a special time in Milwaukee modified racing and each driver had a nickname — the Mouse, Donald Duck, the Rabbit, the Wiener Dog — and carried the cartoon figure painted on the car. Schill was Tweetie Bird. At the end of each year they traveled as a caravan to Escanaba, Michigan, and Sault Sainte Marie,

Canada. The Canadians shook their heads in amazement as they watched the "Milwaukee Monsters" party all night and then race the next day.

It was also a special time for Al's wife and constant companion at the races, Gwen, whom he began to date at age 9 and married at age 18. At first her racing involved driving the 1955 sportsman from their home down the road to Al's father's salvage yard. Soon she was racing and winning on the same road against her husband in his brother Ted's car. At the track she hot lapped Al's car and loaded it on the truck.

Soon she had her own 1957 Ford powderpuff car that was painted green with flowers all over it to race at Wilmot and Lake Geneva. Then came a 1956 Chevrolet painted identical to Al's modified. In her years of racing, she seldom finished below third.

The high point came one night in a scheduled 10-lap race between Gwen and Al at Rockford, Illinois, in which they gave Gwen a straightaway lead. Figuring a car was a car, Al mashed the gas pedal to the floor in his borrowed racer and promptly crashed in turn one when the brakes failed to respond. Gwen won the race and a trophy. Al got a crying towel.

1972 was a turning point in Schill's career. His father had passed away and Al needed every cent that he could find to purchase his father's salvage yard. He sold everything he had, including two Frings chassis, to make the down payment.

However, Al's desire to race remained. Lacking money, Schill decided to build a 1957 Chevrolet sportsman car to race at Hales Corners. As luck would have it, Hales Corners switched from modifieds to late models. Schill removed the 1957 body from its chassis, put on a 1972 Nova body and went on to win the late model championship. His crew chief for that year and every year until 1983, when he joined the Bobby Allison team as crew chief, was Jim Fennig.

In 1973, Schill continued to race the same car on dirt and purchased a Frings chassis to run on the pavement. In 1974, Jeff Fennig, Jim's brother and a talented man in his own right, joined the Schill crew. His abilities as a body man made Schill's race cars award winners in appearance. Fennig was responsible for the body and paint scheme of Schill's cars and began to manufacture pit accessories for racing on a national level.

In 1975, Schill rented a USAC car from Jack Bowsher for a singular appearance on the USAC circuit in a 250-mile race at Milwaukee. A bad decision on tires in the late stages of the race kept him from finishing third. Bowsher had dropped out of the race and decided to bring Schill in and replace his tires with the softer compound that he had been running. "We shouldn't have done it because the track was getting slick," says Schill, "and the harder tire I had on was a better tire for the surface." Schill finished fourth.

One of the stars and veterans of the Milwaukee area, Wally Jors, died of a heart attack in 1976. What started as a casual remark to Gwen about buying Jors' car while they were eating lunch one day turned into reality. "I'll never forget it," says Gwen. "Al brought the car home on Friday night and we stripped the enamel paint off with paint stripper. By race time Saturday the race car wasn't lettered, but it was painted."

Schill was assisted by Jors' brother-in-law and father-in-law for the remainder of the season. "We finished second in the points," says Al. "If we had raced the full season in the car, we might have won the championship."

As it was, Schill won championships at Hales Corners in 1977, 1978, and 1979. At the same time he was track champion at Cedarburg in 1977 and 1979. His main competitors were Whity Harris and the legendary Miles "The Mouse" Milius. During those years the trio was known as "The Big Three."

The ARTGO circuit attracted Schill's attention in 1982 and he steadily progressed from seventh place that year to a third place finish in the point standings in 1985, the last year that he ran the full circuit.

197

Of all his ARTGO memories, the one that stands out is a wreck that occurred in 1983 at Fort Wayne, Indiana. The feature race was just getting under way when Schill got off the track on the back straight. When he tried to correct the car, it slid backwards into turn three and hit an implement tire with such force that the car went 25 feet in the air. The car flew 40 feet before landing on its roof. The right side of the roll cage collapsed. "By the time the dust cleared and the safety crew got there, I was gone. If there is one thing I am afraid of it is fire and I wasn't waiting around to see if one was going to break out."

In 1984, Schill won the 200-lap National Short Track Championship at Rockford by leading the race from start to finish. The first ten cars were inverted and since Schill had timed in tenth he got the pole. He led the first 100 laps and then had to nervously sit out a break before the second 100 laps were run. He again took the lead and became the first driver to ever win by leading from start to finish.

As in 1972, when Schill purchased his father's salvage yard, 1985 was again a year in which he chose to curtail his racing schedule to meet the demands of an ever growing business. He attended two or three auctions a week, processed 2,600 cars a year at the yard, and sold 4,000 tons of metal a year. As a result he no longer campaigned the whole ARTGO circuit, but centered his attention once again on Hales Corners and Slinger, a combination of dirt and pavement.

"How do I do it? It is just a matter of touch. My success at both tracks," he said, "was due to those early years of six nights a week where we switched back and forth from one type of surface to the other using the same car."

Al Schill had that special touch, on dirt or pavement.

TED MUSGRAVE

Illinois driver finds action in Wisconsin

After years of struggling, 1987 was a season in which Ted Musgrave would reach a new plateau. The break came when Mike Randerson, of Rander-Car Chassis, suggested Ted as a possible driver to Terry Baker. Baker had got his start as a team owner in 1984 when, after the Miller 200 in Milwaukee, he walked out of the stands and asked Ed Evans what it would take to run up front. In 1985 Baker and Evans teamed up to run a 1985 Firebird on the ASA circuit. When the season was over they were 15th in the point standings.

Ted Musgrave

Evans retired and Baker asked Bobby Dotter to be his driver. Howard Lettow became the crew chief and Gene Mathu became the engine sponsor. "We went out and ran very well," Baker says. "When we ran, we ran as fast as anyone. We were Goliath-slayers if you will." But the team still needed a winner.

When Dotter moved to the Gunderman Team, it left the opening that Ted Musgrave would fill. He sold all of his equipment, except his motor, to his brother Tom, and put all of his eggs in one basket. He had never had more than one car, now he had three Buick LaSabres.

He had always worked alone or with the help of his wife, Debbie; now he had a crew chief who had been around the circuit and knew how to set up the car for each race. Instead of being under a race car frantically changing parts in order to make a race, he was now told to get a haircut and present a clean-cut image to the press and public.

For Ted Musgrave, 1987 was a year of transition. But he lived up to the challenge. Still there was reason to wonder as the season got under way. Ted's first race at Rockford was a disaster. A loose seat belt forced him to start in back and when Bob Senneker blew a radiator hose Ted drove right into the water. But the rest of the season was a great one.

Musgrave won at Milwaukee, Birmingham and Huntsville. He finished second at Sanair, Cayuga, Calgary, Milwaukee and Indianapolis. He was third at Kaukauna, Sandusky and LaCrosse. In the 25 races he entered he was running at the end of 21 of them. As a result he was fifth in the ASA points and second in SCC points. At the beginning of the summer the goal was rookie of the year on the ASA circuit. At the end of the summer he was the rookie of the year and a deserving one.

Ted got his start in the Chicago area. His father, Elmer, was a well known driver in that area for over a quarter of a century. He raced modifieds in the slam bang contests at Soldiers Field and O'Hare, as well as Wilmot and Waukegan. Later he advanced to late models and asphalt. "I was really young at the time," says Ted, "But I can still remember sitting in the infield at Milwaukee and watching him race against drivers like Paul Goldsmith. He finally retired so he could help my older brother, Tom, and I get started. He was always on the scene for the first three years of my career. He built my engines and his advice helped me get a sound start. Then he let me race on my own."

Tom Musgrave, who lived with his parents at the time in Mundelein, Illinois, ran his first race at Waukegan in 1977 at the age of 18. "My brother bought Dave Watson's car and I inherited it — his 1967 Ford Galaxy. I immediately took it apart and turned it into a 1967 Ford Torino, which I raced for one year. It was a tank, but it was safe and, looking back, I needed that safety factor. I made some mistakes in that rookie year." Not enough to keep him from being name Waukegan's rookie of the year.

Ted began the next season in a Ford Mustang that he and his dad built in the off season. Applying all of their own knowledge, as well as a few tips from Dick Trickle, who was driving Fords at the time, made the car a fast one. Ted raced the car as a Mustang, a Camaro and again as a Mustang for three years in an ever expanding area. By 1979 he was a familiar face on the tough and demanding CWRA circuit and finished seventh in the point standings. He also established a Waukegan track record of 12:53.

"My parents and I decided to move to Wisconsin because you could race five nights a week. I raced at LaCrosse, Wausau, Grundy, the Dells and Waukegan each week. Those grueling years were a major step in my becoming a race driver."

In 1981, Musgrave would finish second to Alan Kulwicki in the points race at Kaukauna by two points. He also had an opportunity to drive a car prepared by Jimmy Back at the Odessa, Missouri I-70 Speedway and would finish 10th in the race.

The highlight of the 1982 season on the CWRA circuit was the winning of the Holiday 50 at Capital Speedway. Ted also had fast time five nights in a row at Kaukauna and was leading in the points race when his wrist was battered in a wreck. He returned the next week with a cast and a special arm support built in the car. He would finish the season third in points.

In 1983, Ted won 10 features and finished second on numerous occasions on the CWRA circuit. He again won the Holiday 50, the Triple Hot Dog Dash at Wisconsin Dells, and the Race of Champions at Capital

Speedway's Oktober Nationals.

In 1984, Ted Musgrave reached another plateau as a stock car driver. The accumulated years of experience and his own hard work, sacrifice, and determination gave him the ability to win with consistency on the toughest circuit in the Midwest. Ted won seven features at Capital Speedway, one of them the prestigious Fourth of July Holiday 100. He set fast time at the track in over half of the events he entered including the Oktober Nationals. He won two features at Wausau, two at LaCrosse and two at Wisconsin Dells. He capped the season by timing in fourth at the Minnesota State Fair and leading the race until six laps from the end when a collision with Jim Sauter eliminated him. Ted had proven he was a quality driver. All that was needed was an offer by a car owner or sponsor that would give him the ability to display those talents on a wider circuit.

The season of 1985 found Ted still struggling to make it on his own. Funds ran out and his season ended early. "I'll just have to start cutting wood early," he said, referring to the cold Wisconsin winters.

In 1986, Ted was back with a new car that contained a number of his own experimental ideas. He set numerous fast times and had a number of dash, heat, and feature wins. His finest hour that summer came when he won the Firecracker 100 on the Fourth of July at Capital Speedway. Despite starting the season in June, Ted still finished 10th in CWRA points.

In 1987, he was offered a ride by Terry Baker. Ted made the most of it and became the ASA rookie of the year.

Throughout the years, Ted has had the support of his parents and brother, Tom. He also found additional support and strength in the girl who would become his wife, Deborah Pantle. They met while traveling back and forth to Waukegan on Sunday nights. "She was a friend of a friend of my father who needed a ride back to Illinois on Sunday nights. First we talked, then we dated, and you know how that goes ..." says Ted.

The newly married couple settled in Grand Marsh, where Debbie trained and showed horses while Ted raced. They had two sons, Justin and Ted, Jr.

One time, Debbie was on her way to the LaCrosse Speedway with Justin when she saw a turtle on the road. Debbie stopped and put the turtle in the box of her Ranchero and proceeded down the road, with Justin watching the turtle crawl around in the back of the truck through the back window. All of a sudden Justin was screaming loudly, "Mom, stop. Mom, stop."

"What is wrong?" asked Debbie.

"Mom, you are going too fast. You just blew the head, the arms and the legs right off the turtle. The only thing left is the box he came in."

"Someday Justin is going to be the terror of the tracks," Ted said. "He has no fear of speed. The faster he can go on a motorcycle or a car the better. He has had a four-wheeler up to 85 and was trying to get still more speed out of the throttle. He gives me a heart attack, but he will be a tough one."

Ted Musgrave made his Winston Cup debut in 1990, when he was asked to fill in after the tragic death of Rich Vogler. He has raced on the NASCAR circuit ever since.

Justin Musgrave went on to race light trucks while Ted Musgrave Jr. raced on the ASA circuit.

JOE SHEAR

Proud driver
to the end

Midget driver Kevin Olson told me that Joe Shear would sit in the upper row of the bleachers on the first turn of Angell Park when he wasn't racing himself. I looked there often, but I never saw him.

Joe Shear

Shear, who passed away in March 1998, following a three-year battle with cancer, was the consummate short track racer. "He had life his way," says his wife Connie. "When his employer put in a time clock, Joe punched out and never went back. He was a 'day sleeper,' getting up at 10. He would start work on the car at two in the afternoon and stay at it until late. He did one thing to the max. He didn't jump to other things. I think there is a lesson there for all of us."

In Shear's basement is a black-and-white checkered floor, and trophies stand four and five deep along the wall. Shear's obituary estimated that he had won 350 times. Said Fred Nielsen, Joe's car owner from 1975 to 1984 and 1986 to 1994 as well as his best friend: "We won 250 races as a team and the total is probably more like 600."

Shear was a quiet kind of guy, the sort announcers

hate to interview. "There were times especially in his early career,"' Connie remembers, "when he would not talk to a soul. He would go to the track, unload the car, set a track record, win the feature and leave."

He was that way as a child, says his mother, Jeane. "His first sentence, a complete 'Let me out' when the screen door was hooked, astounded all of us. He refused to go to kindergarten. He fussed and cried the whole way there on the first day."

The trophies and the pictures on the wall are arranged according to the years they were won. They begin with his go-kart trophies. Next is the one from Rockford Speedway for Outstanding Mechanic of 1962.

His father, the late Art Shear, won championships at Rockford in 1951, 1962 and 1965. Underage, Joe would sneak into the pits to help him. He was rookie of the year in 1964 and won his first career victory on his birthday, May 8, 1965. By 1972, he had won six consecutive late model championships at the track. His first Rockford National Short Track Championship also came in 1972.

Joe Shear won more than 30 track and series championship trophies. Although he was known as a pavement driver, two of those championships were at Freeport, Illinois, on the dirt. "He had 11 consecutive wins at one point," says Connie. "The other drivers hated to see him coming into the pits."

While Dick Trickle holds the record for ARTGO wins with 68, Joe finished his career with 58. He won ARTGO championships in 1986 and 1989.

During Daytona's Speedweeks he won the Volusia County championship in 1990 and the New Smyrna title in 1988 and 1989. Shear won the Red, White, and Blue Series at Kaukauna in 1979, 1987 and 1988. He won the Slinger Nationals four times and the first Wisconsin Short Track Series in 1994.

His most cherished trophies, those from the most prestigious races, stand on a table in the center of the room. Shear always wanted to win at the Milwaukee mile and finally did in 1986 (the ARTGO Midwest Challenge) and in 1994, on his 50th birthday, in the ASA Badger and 150. In that one, Shear was leading when he pitted, came out 18th, and within 22 laps was back in the lead.

"Of all the races we won together, that was my favorite," says Fred Nielsen. "We had tried so hard in the past, even going through the fence and into the grandstands in turn four."

Shear won not only on his driving ability but also because he was meticulous at building and maintaining the car. "I chose him as my driver because he was the best available," says Nielsen, "and he was the best finish person and fabricator there was."

"He was meticulous," says Connie.

Shear built his first race car at age 16 and went on to build virtually every car he ever raced. In 1994 he drove a house car for Wayne Lensing's Lefthander Chassis with motors by Jerry Lemke of JAMR. Both Lensing and Lemke treasured his input.

Shear won 11 of 17 races in the Lefthander in 1994 But serious trouble lay ahead. In January 1995, doctors removed two tumors from Shear's throat. Doctors believed they had removed everything, but recommended radiation. Instead Joe went through a three-week metabolic treatment in Mexico. When he felt better, Shear didn't even follow through on that. Later, he admitted he was sorry he didn't listen to the doctors. That spring, Shear amazed everyone by showing up for the Rockford opener and setting fast time.

Throughout his three-year battle with cancer he never lost his ability to drive a race car. In fact, he said he always felt best after a race. The most painful part of a race was putting a helmet on. "He had a high tolerance of pain," Connie says.

She recalls the time he broke his leg racing at the Minnesota State Fair. "He used me as a crutch after he got out of the car. We went to the hospital, but he wouldn't let them put a cast on. Instead they wrapped it with tape."

"Larry Detjens' and Dick Trickle's crews as well as our own worked to get the car back in shape," Fred Nielsen adds. "Joe drove it to a third-place finish using his right leg and complaining on the radio every time he forgot and hit the brake with his left foot. The next week he drove I-70. He never did have a cast put on it."

1996 was one of the best years in Shear's career. He won eight ARTGO races and five out of six specials at Kaukauna. He could feel the cancer returning in May but chose to race. The doctors could wait until the season was over.

On February 7, 1997, Joe had surgery to remove lymph nodes and muscles from both sides of his neck. Five weeks of radiation followed. He was back at Rockford in the spring. For the first time, he was too weak to hang the body on the car. His crew did work Shear normally did himself. But he never gave up.

Despite failing health, Shear won four of his last five races. In the final race of his career at the LaCrosse Oktoberfest, his car was two-tenths of a second faster than anyone else but the motor blew. The crew changed the motor, and the second one blew, too. Then Brad Wagner offered Joe a ride. He took the car from 25th to fourth. "Ten more laps and we would have won," a crew member contends.

Shear's final trophy, which stands at the end of the third wall, was earned in his next-to-last race: Rockford's National Short Track Championship. It was his eighth win in that event.

"I was his spotter," says Connie. "I tried to keep him out of trouble. He knew how to drive. On that day, I was his cheerleader. For 50 laps, he was stuck in fifth behind John Lemke. Finally, I told God that if He wanted Joe to win, He had to do something. Joe got underneath him and went on to victory. I knew we were making a memory. When it was over and he got out of the car, the roar of the crowd sounded like angels. He told me he never would have won if it hadn't been for my cheering him on."

In November 1997, Joe went back to the doctor. The doctor put his stethoscope down and with a solemn face said to Joe: "I hate to tell you this, but it is back."

"That was the first time Joe faced the reality that cancer would take his life," says Connie. "On the way home he made me promise not to tell a soul."

"I'll tell them when I am ready," Joe said. "I don't want to be treated differently."

"He was never ready," Connie continues. "Finally I had to get Hospice to help me. The next day was our son Steve's birthday, and we agreed when everyone gathered it would be an appropriate time. We were all there when he asked if I was going to tell them. He had to go to the bathroom."

The people in that room became the center of what was left of Joe Shear's life — his wife Connie, five children and his friends. "Racing was no longer important to him, just his family," says Steve. "If you take the passage from Corinthians about love is patient, love is kind, and put his name in every time it says 'love,' that was who he became over the years."

"It was an honor and a privilege to share his life," says Connie. "I can't describe how much we loved him... I loved him. In November, he said he wanted to race one more year. In January, I told him he would never be able to. He knew it, but he still had hope.

"He was not afraid of death. A born-again Christian, he believed that he was going to heaven and that I will follow him some day.

"If there is anything good about his death, it was that he passed away at the height of his career. Even though he didn't care, he left the public eye while doing his best."

Joe never mowed the grass, vacuumed the floor or planted flowers, but he gave his family other things: a dry sense of humor, ping-pong tournaments on holidays and basketball in the driveway after the racing season. He was the roughest player and had a wicked hook shot.

A young Joe Shear waits for introduction at Wisconsin Dells.

Joe loved his fans, but Jason was special. He also had cancer and had undergone chemotherapy. His family made sure he was done with his treatments in time to be at the track and watch Joe race. "I've got the same thing as Joe," he would say. He was the only person, with the exception of the crew, to ever put on a headset and talk to Joe during a race.

"When Jason was through with chemotherapy," says Connie, "they gave him a victory party at McDonald's, but Joe was too sick to go. At Joe's funeral I hugged him and told him he had to grow up to be strong, to be a race driver."

In the final days of his life, Joe Shear, with a weak, raspy voice, asked Connie if he could go down to the race room.

"Joe," Connie said, "you can't go down there. How will I ever get you up the steps?" But he had to go.

"Once there," Connie says, "he walked slowly around the room and looked at the trophies and pictures. He tried to reach out and touch some of them. He knew he was saying good-bye."

DICK TRICKLE

Rising to any challenge

Dick Trickle was still a child when a traveling show came to the small central Wisconsin town of Rudolph. "There was a man in it who could ride a bicycle backwards," Dick recalls, "and it became a challenge to every kid in town." They all tried it, failed and gave up. But not Dick Trickle. He continued trying long after everyone else had given up. Then he went a foot... two feet.

"I'm one of those guys who hangs on and tries and believes he can do things even if he can't. I may not be able to do it today but I will tomorrow. I just never say die. I go after it until I get it," Trickle says as he describes his determination.

Determination is but one of many things that has made Dick Trickle the most successful short track racer in America. The overcoming of obstacles is another. "It seems as if something has always been bucking me," he says.

Adversity began at a very early age when he was playing tag in the rafters of a house that was under construction and fell two floors, landing in the basement and shattering his hip. The recovery period was a long, slow one in which the doctors gave up and sent him home to be an invalid. He defied the odds and began to walk. "You can't tell a kid he is going to be an invalid," says Trickle, who still walks with a slight limp on certain days.

211

Dick Trickle signs autographs at Wisconsin Dells.

When he was nine and in the last stages of recovery, a neighbor took him to his first race at Crown Speedway in Wisconsin Rapids. "When I got there I was flabbergasted. I thought it was the neatest thing. Free shows were nothing compared to it. (In Wisconsin during that era, small towns attracted customers to their stores by showing free movies on the side of a building on a given evening during the summer months.) That race never left my mind until I was 16. I knew I was going to drive a race car when I was 16."

But that brought with it another obstacle — poverty. His father, Lee, had contracted an ear infection which led to more serious problems and he was hospitalized for some 20 years when Dick was growing up. His mother and her five children were on welfare and there was very little money for things like race cars.

At a very early age, Dick was spending his summers with farmers in the area earning money. But another place that he was frequenting was Trickle's Blacksmith Shop on the main street of Rudolph. With his father ill, who had been a partner in the shop, it was run by his uncle Leonard.

"I worked part time at the shop to earn a nickel or dime. At that age, it was mostly sweeping the shop, but I started to play with the welder and soon I could make an arc and then weld.

"I started junking machinery. I saved some things — angle iron, wheels, stanchions out of barns. I was getting a head start for when I would go racing at 16. I didn't have any money, but I had this pile of stuff to build a race car with. It was a hope chest."

"When I turned 16, I let the farmer I was working for keep most the money I earned until fall. That fall I collected my money and went down Main Street wheeling and dealing. I finally bought a 1950 Ford in good condition for $100. It was going to be my street car, but the urge to race got too strong and I cut it up and made a stock car out of it.

"I did run the car a little bit before I cut it up and I ended up drag racing a classmate, Melvin Hunsinger, who had a 1949 Ford. He beat me. It seems kind of dumb that I would make a race car out of a 1950 Ford when I already knew there was a car that could beat me. Eventually, I bought Hunsinger's 1949 Ford for $32.50 and put the motor in my car."

At first, he was the slowest of the slow in a field of 100 cars at Stratford, Wisconsin. He ran that car at the end of 1958 and throughout 1959, then built a 1956 Ford into which he incorporated all of the things he had learned up to that point.

"It would be considered a hobby stock today, but it had a lot of improvements. In fact, the first time out I finished second in the feature at Griffith Park in Wisconsin Rapids without any previous testing. But that second place finish brought with it another obstacle.

"Now they could see I was going to be a real competitor, so they checked and found I was too young to race. I had been racing there two years! I raced elsewhere but had to stop racing there for a whole year and it hurt because it was my home track."

That brought still another obstacle for Trickle to overcome. At the local high school, where he had made the varsity basketball team as a junior, someone commented that this was the same Dick Trickle that had been racing during the summer and he had to be too old to be eligible. When they checked, they indeed found out he was. He had started school late and had lost a year because of his hip injury.

"That was a blow because basketball was a big thing in a town like Rudolph," says Dick. "But I think all of, those childhood obstacles made me tougher. When I couldn't race at Griffith Park, it made me a little fiercer at the other tracks. From then on I was in the feature."

But poverty still remained a factor. Trickle would marry in 1961. His wife, Darlene, still recalls the weekend. The motel room in Merrill, Wisconsin, that Saturday night cost $8. Dick raced at Wausau on Sunday afternoon and Griffith Park on Sunday night. They lived with his grandmother for a while. One of their first homes would be a trailer parked on someone else's property. Some of his first shops had a dirt floor and

During the 1980's, Dick Trickle tested the waters of NASCAR, then decided to stay for a while with the short tracks. As a result, he was billed the winningest short track racer in history.

today he can chuckle about stopping at the local cream-ery to heat a can of water with the steam hose for wash-ing clothes.

After his high school farming experiences, Trickle had two other jobs. One, at Warren Hendrick's Pure Oil Station in Rudolph, not only helped him support his family, but gave valuable experience in working with cars and engines. Hendrick's also sent Trickle to vari-ous schools to help cope with every task that came in the door. "Doing it is learning it," says Trickle of the experience. Trickle worked for Hendrick's 66 hours a week and raced four nights a week. On Tuesday and Thursday, Dick worked for Hendrick's until nine. On the other nights he could bring the car to the shop, but he had to have it out and the shop cleaned by morning.

"I can't say I worked harder for an employer than I ever did for myself. I always gave a day's work for a day's pay. It is harder to work for yourself. If it wasn't for the fact that I love to race so much I don't think I could work as hard as I do. There is some sense there that pushes you to do more and more. Something just clicks when you are doing what you want."

It was hard to be a full-time racer in central Wiscon-sin in those days. "In those days it didn't cost anything to race and the payoffs were fair. You could actually make money racing then and it was to your benefit to be the car owner. Gas was 25 cents a gallon. The parts came out of the junkyard. The tires were $2 apiece and sometimes free if you would take them away. It paid anywhere from $100 to $300 to win a feature. The prob-lem was that it was so seasonal, from May to Septem-ber, and there were seven other months that you had to support a family."

It was while Trickle was working for the local tele-phone company that he made the decision to go rac-ing full time. "One night I came home and told my wife that I had been up those poles for two years and I never was comfortable with heights. She said I should either quit or tell them to let me do something else. They let me do other things. Two or three years later, I came home again and told my wife that if I put 100 percent of my effort toward racing, I could probably make a living. She told me to try it. When I told the company, they looked at me like I was a fool. How could anybody in Rudolph make a living racing? Grow up, kid, and quit racing.

"I told my wife I had better make it because I would always be racing and if I didn't I'd just be taking money from elsewhere to race. It was mighty slim for a few years. My wife can stretch a dollar twice as far as anyone or we wouldn't have made it. We didn't necessarily hurt, but if people knew how few dollars we lived on they wouldn't have known how we lived as good as we did. Sometimes I wonder if things weren't better. Now I'm too busy to bowl once a week."

One of the many people who have been a part of Trickle's crew from the very start in Uncle Leonard's shop was Big John (Botcher) who spent every moment that he wasn't working at Consolidated Paper with Trickle.

"Big John worked for my uncle. He had been a pit steward at Crown Speedway and every so often he would come over to the corner of the shop where I was working and offer advice. One day, Uncle Leonard asked him who he was working for. Big John replied that he thought he would mess around with the race car. He was with me 20 years until his health got him. You could almost say his life was lived for me and my car.

"It is funny, but all the years he was with me he knew I didn't have any money. So he must have figured out how much I had by what I would order when we would stop to eat. Whatever I ordered, he ordered."

Through it all, Trickle never saw being poor as a problem. "I don't think it was that bad since I was born and raised poor. Sometimes you wonder if you aren't supposed to be poor. I think your life is as good or better. I have some money now, but if I was rich I don't think my life would be better. It doesn't take money to have a good life. In fact, if some people didn't have so much money they would have a better life."

As a full time racer, Trickle's schedule grew to over 100 programs a year, a schedule he kept for some 15 years. It was at Tomah-Sparta Speedway that Francis Kelly took notice of him. "He watched me race with no money and junk motors. I was always in contention to win, but lost a lot of races because of junk motors. I guess he got sick of it because one day he came over and asked, 'What would it take for you to win?'

"I told him a motor and he told me make up a list of parts. When I showed it to him he asked who was going to build it. I told him I could, but I was a junkyard mechanic. I suggested Alan Kulwicki's father, Jerry, who was with Norm Nelson at the time. Kulwicki built it and I ran it for two years without a problem. That gave me a lot more time to work on chassis."

A turning point in Trickle's career came in 1966 when he entered the first National Short Track Championship race at Rockford Speedway. He recalls that, "The cars in that area were fancier and looked like they were ahead of us. They didn't treat us bad, but they sort of giggled at us kids with the rat cars. After two days, they looked differently at those rat cars. I won and pocketed $1,645. Before, I questioned spending the money to travel that far. But if you could win, that was a different story."

In 1971, Trickle won 41 races. In 1972, he set a record with 67 victories. In 1973, he won 57 races. "The Ford big blocks made me," Dick says. "I had them down pat. Then they put the weight-per-cubic-inch rule in and I suffered some of the lowest moments in my career in 1975 and 1976. Fords almost broke me. I couldn't get any pieces for racing at my level. It took two years of hard labor and depleting my funds to realize I couldn't do this anymore.

"I told myself either I had to change my program or get out of racing. I was working day and night and going broke. I was never ready to race because I was too busy. I decided to go with GM and see if I couldn't swing a deal with an engine builder. My first choice was Prototype. With a little help from a person who worked there, Ron Neal was willing to make a deal.

"Then I bought a car from BEMCO for $13,000, which was a lot in those days. With my word that I would pay for it before September, I won 35 or 40 races that summer and had it paid for by July. We got through those years before 1976. I supported my family. I learned a lot but what we've got today we gained from 1977 till now."

The winner of numerous ASA and ARTGO titles claims as one of his best memories the winning of the World Crown 300 in Georgia in 1983 and being declared the king of the short trackers. "It took three weeks of preparation and a lot of determination. It was the biggest payday of my career up to that point."

Asked why he has been so successful, Trickle responds, "I think I had certain engineering and mechanical abilities born into me. I think certain people and families have certain areas where they perform better. It just happens that my areas involve racing. It is something that comes pretty natural to me. If I was going to be a literature teacher, I would have to work very hard. Reading and writing is OK, but the biggest waste of time is a poem. But it is real easy for me to take a radio or engine apart and put it together or design a better motor, A-frame or camber gauge. That is a matter of common sense to me.

"That plus my never-say-die attitude. When you back your car into the wall and it is junk, bent in the middle, and your back and ribs are hurting, it is a low feeling. You try not to show it, but it is there. The next morning you unload the car and start again.

"Another thing might be that I gave up all security and went racing 110 percent. I went into it with tunnel vision and cut everything else out of my life. I could see you couldn't do it as a part-time racer. The only other way is to become a doctor and get a good practice and buy everything to become a good racer. But then the money will make you look better than you are. If you take someone like myself, who came from the bottom up, and the person with a lot of money and make them run with the same opportunities and cash flow and equipment, the guy who started on the bottom is going to come out on top."

Another reason Trickle was America's most successful short track racer is that is where he stayed so many years. "When 1 was young and bold, I had a wife and two children to support. I was taught that it was the man who was the head of the family and it was his duty to support that family. I would have dug ditches to support them if that is what it took. Most of those going to NASCAR today are going without a family to support.

"I made some early changes. I went and ran USAC with my own dollars and was rookie of the year. I spent a lot of my short track winnings on USAC. I went to Daytona with my own money. What happened was I was so busy racing that I couldn't see around me. I was working 16 hours a day and I wasn't thinking ahead. Then it came to a point that I got good enough at it that why should I leave being successful to be a mid-pack runner there? Their lives aren't any better than mine and I'm a freer man."

For Trickle, life has always had its challenges and obstacles, but there has always been room for fun. "I believe life is 50 percent pleasure and 50 percent pain. If you can move it up to 60 percent pleasure you are doing good."

In the old days, there were places like the Blue Tiger in LaCrosse. "That is the place my wife didn't like. One evening, five Green Berets were visiting from nearby Camp McCoy and arm wrestling in a corner of the establishment. Francis Kelly went over and told them he knew someone who could beat them. I took on the two toughest and won. They didn't get mad, in fact they put me on their shoulders and carried me around the bar."

Grubba

Then there was a Saturday morning when the USAC race got rained out in Memphis, Tennessee. "Naturally we were all staying at the same hotel which happened to be half filled with people from a dog show. By noon, there were rooms with bath tubs filled with ice and beer.

"By seven in the evening, everyone had had enough, but you couldn't tell them that. There was a big rock down by the pool and Joe Frazon worked for an hour and a half to get it in the pool. I think the management knew it was the race people and not the dog people. They threatened to call the cops if things didn't quiet down. The noise persisted and then somebody got the bright idea to go out in the parking lot where all the dog pens were and turn them loose. In 15 minutes there were 35 dogs running all over the parking lot and up and down the hallways.

"Pretty soon a paddy wagon comes and cops are going up and down the halls, grabbing guys and putting them in the paddy wagon. They had me against the wall, but somehow I got away and ran out and crawled under my truck. They knew what direction I'd headed, but when they came I grabbed the drive shaft and pulled myself up out of view.

"I could see them bringing guys out. What I didn't know was that when they were gone, I could have run over and opened the paddy wagon door. They got a lot of people including Bay Darnell and his elderly sponsor, who were innocently sitting in their room watching TV when a few guys ducked in to hide. No one got released until morning."

The story Dick loves to tell dates back to the days when he was racing snowmobiles and they were in Portland, Maine, at Scarborough Downs, where harness racing is the normal attraction. The track put on a big lobster feed on Saturday night for all the drivers and crews.

As others headed home, Dick and four other drivers spotted several sleds used for safety and towing. Soon they were racing them in the dim moonlight. By the time

**In 2000, Dick Trickle was sponsored by
Schneider Trucking of Wisconsin.**

they got done, everyone else was gone and they didn't
have a ride back to the motel, which was about 20 miles
away.

There were some big county trucks around, but a
search turned up no keys. Then Dick spotted an ambulance and the keys were in it.

They all jumped in and took off with Dick as the
driver. One person had to keep the windows from
steaming because of a faulty heater core. Another operated the lights and sirens.

Halfway into town, they went over an overpass as a
squad car went beneath it. "It kept right on going," said
Dick. "They must not pay any attention to one another.

"When we got to the hotel I saw Ed Schibiski's six-
wheel truck parked with its nose against the hotel. I

drove the hood of the ambulance right under the truck, got out and locked it up. The next morning I looked out the window from the third floor and there was a crowd standing around the ambulance. Ed is trying to figure how to get his truck out.

"I laughed a little, showered and walked down and unlocked the ambulance and threw my helmet and suit in and drove off as if it was nothing out of the ordinary."

Dick Trickle said, "I never look at the purse. My wife does. I come to race. The only time I ever looked at the purse was before the World Crown 300 in Georgia in 1983. It was the biggest purse I ever raced for, $50,000. 1 spent a month preparing the car. If anyone did anything on the car, I did it over."

Trickle has this philosophy: "Usually a man who works hard, plays hard. The drivers I grew up with were a group of assertive, hard-working, very determined people At 10 p.m. you just don't wipe out these efforts. What got us there kept us there; just because the races were over didn't mean pulling the shades and going to bed. You are still pumped up. What are you going to do, stop at a corner church?

"Well, we went down to the corner pub to socialize. Fortunately, they closed at 1 so we did get home. Enjoying yourself, whether it is over a brew or a game of bingo, is better than laying back and pouting or watching TV.

"It was just the type of people more than anything. We grew up in the beer bar days. Those were the fifties, my boy. People were pretty lively. They talk about the thirties, which I don't know about, but I'll tell you one thing. I think those fifties are going to be around for a long time. It was an era. What we did was the common thing.

"I've done a lot, but I dwell on where I am going. Yesterday is gone. Each year is a new one. There is new equipment, new tracks, and new challenges. Who can say that my career has peaked? I certainly don't think that way."

CONRAD MORGAN
Apples don't fall far

L ike Adam and Eve, it began with an apple. In 1966, late model driver Conrad Morgan of Dousman was towing his race car to nearby Jefferson Speedway. As he went around a curve the hitch came loose and the race car took off and came to rest under a farmer's apple tree.

"There it was," Conrad remembers, "Sifting against the tree with apples bouncing all over. The farmer was really hot!"

Like Adam and Eve, Morgan was banished from the orchard. The rookie driver continued down the road and by the end of the summer he was sure he hadn't left but found paradise. In that

Conrad Morgan

first summer of racing at Jefferson, which had just become a paved quarter mile, he won a heat race, $12, and a trophy. Morgan figured he was on his way to making a fortune.

While he may not have made the millions of an Earnhardt or a Gordon, Morgan has established himself as one of the toughest racers in the Midwest.

"When I realized that I would not be the next Dale Earnhardt, it took the pressure off me. I could have fun racing."

It was 10 years before Morgan won his first track championship at Lake Geneva in 1977. Like apples from a tree, the titles have been falling his way ever since as he, for no reason he can think of, defies the aging process.

223

Grubba

Morgan won two more titles at Lake Geneva in 1978 and 1980. During those early years he added another championship at the quarter mile in Columbus. Then he began to concentrate on the half mile at Madison and the high-banked quarter mile at Slinger. At Madison, Morgan won titles in 1983 and 1984.

It is the 1984 battle with Steve Holzhausen that slicks in Morgan's memory. Holzhausen was coming on strong at the end of the season and trailed Morgan by just a few points going into the final night.

"It was raining when we got to the track," says Morgan. "He was getting faster at the end of the season and I was getting slower. If it hadn't rained I might not have won the championship. After the races were canceled and the title was determined we were still standing around when it quit raining. We had a five lap grudge race and Holzhausen won."

But it is at Wayne Erickson's world's fastest quarter mile in Slinger that Morgan has dominated in recent years, winning titles in 1992, 1994, 1995, 1997, 1998 and 1999. It is no small feat since the toughest competition in Wisconsin gathers there every Sunday night.

The most memorable of the Slinger titles was in 1994 when Morgan missed a race early in the summer and trailed Al Schill, Sr., who has won 17 track titles including six at Slinger, all summer.

"Al probably doesn't like to remember it, but I went into the final night 20 points behind. I ended up winning the championship."

In his strongest showing at Slinger, 1997, Morgan won the championship by over 300 points. "The car ran great all year. I had one DNF, one fifth, and one fourth. All the rest of the feature finishes were third or better."

Besides his championships within the state of Wisconsin Morgan has proven himself beyond the state lines.

In 1989, Morgan ran the Big Ten Series at Concord, North Carolina, part time and then returned to run it full time in 1990. He missed the championship by eight points when he erroneously thought a right front tire was going flat. By the time he recovered, it was too late to overtake the leader. Morgan did win the series 200-lap Fourth of July race.

In 1990, Morgan and his crew also traveled to Phoenix for the Copper World Classic. He finished fourth behind Ken Schroeder, Junior Hanley, and Rick Carelli.

Morgan has had a few bad apples drop in his lap. Twice he has hit the end of the wall at the exit into the pits. At Slinger, he and Joel Laufer got together between turns one and two. Laufer went through the exit. At Rockford, the car ahead of him hit the large implement tire guarding the end of the pit exit wall and knocked it straight in the air. Morgan hit the end of the wall with such force that he didn't remember anything for two days.

At Madison, Scoff Ollerman blew an engine and Morgan, followed by Scott Wimmer, was the first person to hit the oil. "I hit the brakes and it was like I speeded up another 100 mph. The impact even broke the intake manifold." Again Morgan escaped serious injury, but doesn't remember going to work the next day.

What Morgan does remember are the good times and, now in his fifties, they show no sign of coming to an end.

"I wonder about it," Morgan says. "I don't know why I am still winning, but I do wonder. I look at Petty, Waltrip, and Earnhardt and all of a sudden it seems done."

When it is done for him, Conrad Morgan will have three sons involved in the sport. Two, Justin and Ryan, are presently crew members. A third, Donavan, is doing very well as a driver, proof that good apples never fall far from the tree.

"Go tell Dad I just got fast time," Donavan said recently at Slinger.

Told that Conrad responded, "Go tell Donavan the money is in the feature." He should know. He has won them.

KULWICKI, MARCIS, SAUTER, KENSETH
NASCAR heroes

• ALAN KULWICKI

For Alan Kulwicki the step up to the NASCAR circuit was a matter of perseverance and timing. "It has been a matter of meeting the challenges that came up along the way," says Alan. "The first time I went to an ASA

race at I-70 I was half afraid, but I finished third. Another risk involved running the ASA circuit. I could have run out of money, but I finished fourth in the points. Moving to the NASCAR circuit has involved some of the same risks, but it was something I wanted to do."

It was also a matter of timing. "Everyone says you should have a sponsor and a team when you try to break into NASCAR. When I

Alan Kulwicki

ran five races at the end of 1985, I felt I could do it. Two and one half months later I didn't have anything. I went to Daytona and didn't make the show. I could have failed. I took the chance. I looked at the drivers coming up and felt that was the year to make a move even if it meant doing it with less money. Timing is critical. That first year was enjoyable. No one expected me to do anything. Anything I accomplished was looked at as overachieving."

Kulwicki was NASCAR Rookie of the Year in 1986 and went on to become Winston Cup champion in 1992. He

Wausau native Dave Marcis raced as one of the top independents on the NASCAR circuit.

was killed April 1, 1993, in a plane crash.

• DAVE MARCIS

Dave Marcis has always loved the life of an independent. It has been a life of hard work and deep personal satisfaction. The half-mile at Richmond, Virginia, has been the scene of both sacrifice and life's greatest moment.

In 1979, Marcis was returning home from a race in Richmond when a gas line on his tow truck broke. The gas poured onto the truck's muffler and soon there were flames everywhere. "Frank Young from Shoney's was with me, and we couldn't even get out the right hand door. We had to jump out the left side. Great way to treat a sponsor, right?"

Dave risked his life trying to unhitch the trailer and race car. "It was dangerous, but my car was back there and that's how I make my living."

A person with a four wheel drive finally helped Dave pull the race car out of danger. "We saved the race car, but we lost the truck, all my equipment and a spare engine. It was a $60,000 loss, and I didn't have insurance. I just couldn't afford it. It was taking every cent I had to operate. When you are an independent a lot of things happen to you."

But good things also happen if one keeps working and Richmond is also the site of one of Marcis' best days as an independent. In February 1982, Dave Marcis was a lap down in the Richmond 400 when the leader, Joe Ruttman, spun. Marcis passed him and got his lap back. Then the three drivers that were still ahead of Marcis pitted. As Marcis assumed the lead it began to rain. "I wasn't praying for rain, but I told the guys when I got out of the car (during the break before the race was cancelled) that if the good Lord wanted to help an independent, this was his chance." Eventually, with darkness setting in, the race was called. Marcis, who had not won in five years, was declared the winner.

"It was one of my greatest moments in racing," Dave recalls. "I had even built my own engine for that race."

• JIM SAUTER

Jim Sauter began his racing career in 1964 in the modified division at Raceway Park in Savage, Minnesota. The following year he switched to the late model division and began his move up the ladder as one of

the Midwest's top drivers. Sauter moved to Wisconsin and in 1971 his short track career reached new heights when he drove a Larry Wehr's sponsored Dave Marcis Chevelle to victory in the North Star 500 at the Minnesota State Fair. "It was the days of the factory Fords and Chrysler products," recalls Jim, "and all the drivers like Ramo Stott were there. We beat them bad. But the funny thing about that race was the fact that we had a barn full of

Jim Sauter

various brands of tires that we wanted to use up and ended up with Goodyear on the outside and Firestone on the inside for no other reason than that. Everyone thought it must be the hot tip and even Ramo Stott copied us."

But the biggest day of Sauter's racing career occurred in 1978 when Dave Marcis called him from Daytona and asked him to drive his Dodge in the ARCA 200. The race was a thriller. Bruce Hill and Sauter crashed on the last lap as they fought for the lead. Hill ended up in the wall and Sauter went on to win. "Up until then," Jim says, "I never dreamed I would race on the NASCAR circuit. It wasn't on my list of things to do. Now I know the challenge is here. The teams are awesome. It appeals to me."

• MATT KENSETH

"If you don't feel like you are ready, we don't have to go to Talladega," Busch Series team owner Robbie Reiser told his rookie driver, Matt Kenseth. Perhaps Reiser was thinking of his own past experiences, one which was a trip to the hospital in the back of an ambulance after an especially fearsome wreck at Talladega. Then too, before Kenseth got the seat, Reiser had been mostly straightening out race cars. "If you don't feel like you are ready...."

"No! No! I-I want to go," declared the 24-year-old Kenseth, who had been making a name for himself on the short tracks.

Reiser, from Allentown, Wisconsin, and Kenseth had been together for just one week.

Kenseth started 1997 driving mainly in local events for Jerry Gunderman, whose other drivers had included Bobby Allison, Mark Martin and Ted Musgrave. Kenseth qualified third and finished second at Kealy, North Carolina. The next weekend he crashed during a Hooter's race at Rougement, North Carolina and was on his way home when Reiser called. Reiser's driver, Tim Berner, had been hurt in an accident and Reiser needed someone to take his place. Although Kenseth had driven in just one race in the Busch Series, Reiser offered him the job. Not long ago, both Reiser and Kenseth were Wisconsin area drivers.

"Matt and I used to have some fierce races against each other," said Reiser. "I needed someone who understood race cars the way I understood them. I knew he could drive and he could talk to me in a manner I could understand."

Reiser told Kenseth: "You have to be at Nashville for the rookie meeting on Thursday."

In 1993, Kenseth was 21 and racing the local Wisconsin tracks. He's come a long way since then.

In his first run for Raiser and just his second-ever Busch Series start, Kenseth qualified third at Nashville and was running third when he spun in the final laps and finished 11th.

The next race on the schedule was Talladega.

"Except for the fall race at Charlotte in 1996, it was my first time in the draft."

Kenseth remembers. "Before the first practice Robbie told me to be careful. Just go out and ride at the end of a train."

He sure figured it out in a hurry. Kenseth qualified 20th and moved forward 13 spots to finish seventh.

"There I was with Randy LaJoie, Michael Waltrip, Jeff Burton and Mark Martin. I pulled out and Jeff Burton pushed me to the front. I kept going until Reiser came on the radio and told me that if I didn't come in, I would run out of gas. It was the neatest feeling I have ever had in a race car.

"I feel more comfortable in the Busch car than I do in a late model. Drafting is tricky. It is like having a big tractor around the car. When you come upon a car, the tendency is to back off because you think you are going to it. You never touch. You push the car. There is a cushion of air around you."

Kenseth was impressive for the rest of the year. When the season ended, his score card showed a pair of top-five finishes (thirds at Dover and California).

On Feb. 22, 1998, at Rockingham, North Carolina, in his 24th start in the series, Matt Kenseth nudged his way by Tony Stewart on the final turn of the final lap for his first Busch Grand National victory. Afterward Mark Martin said that in his view Kenseth was the next big star. He said Jack Roush should sign him up.

Matt Kenseth

Kenseth's progression from Wisconsin short tracks to the big league has been swift and event-filled. He started his career in 1988 while he was just a 16-year-old sophomore at Cambridge High School.

"My dad bought a car when I was 13 and raced it at Madison," Matt recalls. "Neither of us knew much and it was a learning experience. He continued to race in 1988 and 1989. My first car — what might be considered a sportsman — was a 1981 Camaro that Todd Kropf had driven to championships at Madison and Columbus. On the third night out I won a feature. I ran 15 features in 1983 and won two of them."

"The first night out in the Kropf car Matt won a heat race," says his dad, Roy Kenseth. "The third night he won the feature by holding off two of the best drivers at the track, Pete Moore and Dave Phillips, for 20 laps. Matt was smooth. I knew then he was going to be a racer."

"In 1989, 1 bought a new car and ran at Wisconsin Dells for the points title," Matt continues. "The other drivers were tough competition, but I managed to finish second in points and win eight features. We also ran half a year at Columbus and a half year at Golden Sands plus some races at Slinger."

Kenseth's most memorable night in the 1989 campaign came at Slinger. He and late model driver Ted Musgrave both arrived at the track with ill-handling cars. Both fixed their cars, both got fast time and both won their respective features.

At the end of the season, Matt's dad quit driving, demoralized that his son was faster than he was. "When I saw he could beat me, I quit. I had told him when he was 14, 'You work on the car. I'll drive. In the end you will know more than me.'"

In 1990 Kenseth bought a late model from Richie Bickle, who was making his own presence felt on the Wisconsin short tracks. "I ran Slinger. In the opening race I was following the leader, Tony Strupp. When he had a flat tire I inherited the lead and won the race. I didn't win another feature the rest of the year, but I finished sixth in the points at Slinger and won the rookie-of-the-year title."

Kenseth also continued to broaden his experience by entering 15 ARTGO shows and running 40 features that summer.

The following summer, at age 19, Kenseth won at LaCrosse to become the youngest driver ever to win an ARTGO show, breaking Mark Martin's record. Kenseth did it by passing Joe Shear and Steve Holzhausen, then passing and holding off Steve and Tom Carlson.

1992 was a year to challenge Kenseth's desire. He won just three races and blew more engines than he could count. By the end of the season, he was ready to quit.

"I felt we were at a standstill," he says. "I wasn't gaining. My dad and I had some major discussions at the end of the year. We had to find the dollars for a good program or I told him I would rather not race. It sounds silly. I was only 20 years old.

"Rick Kipley of Kipley Performance probably saved me by putting together a great motor program for us. He loaned us a motor for the final race of the season, the LaCrosse Oktoberfest, and we ran well.

"We built a new car from scratch for the 1993 season, installed a Kipley motor, and ran Madison. We won eight features and finished second in the points."

"We were the little guys on a big street in oval track racing," says Kipley. "We had been building motors for the national pulling circuit and wanted to expand. Roy and Matt were both focused and serious about what they were doing. Matt was a clean-cut guy who had his head on straight, both on and off the track."

Other opportunities presented themselves. Kenseth teamed up with Mike Butz, and though it was a struggle at first, eventually they won some races.

At the end of the season, he and his dad campaigned their own car at Madison, where he won the final Short Track Series Race, LaCrosse, and Odessa, Missouri.

"It gave us a lot of confidence for 1994," Kenseth said. The 1994 and 1995 seasons established Kenseth as a short track star. He ran 60 times in three different rides. Kenseth won track championships at both Madison (where he won 12 of 17 features) and Kaukauna.

Running for the same teams and a similar schedule in 1995, Kenseth successfully defended his titles at Madison and Kaukauna. He also won the Red, White, and Blue Series at Kaukauna.

"We knew by 1995 that Matt had too much talent to be with us for very long," says Patty Butz.

She was right. In 1996, engine builder Carl Wegner got together with Kenseth and they went after a Hooters series late model championship. Wegner liked Kenseth because he worked on his own cars and was quick to learn. He was more than a driver. With Paul Paoli and Paul Christman as crewmen, Kenseth moved to the Charlotte area to work out at Wegner's shop. The plan was to run the Hooters Series, five NASCAR truck races, five Busch races and then, in 1997, the whole Busch Series.

The team won one Hooters race and finished third in the points. They entered the spring race at Charlotte in a car Wegner rented from Bobby Dotter and finished 22nd after starting 30th. The year was a disappointing one because they were unable to attract sponsorship. "I would just as soon forget it," Wegner says.

"It was like 1992," adds Kenseth. "Plans just didn't work. I thought things would be different. Personally, I had moved and was adjusting to being a thousand miles from home."

At the end of the summer, the Wegner/Kenseth team dissolved and Matt went back to Wisconsin searching for another ride. He found one at Jerry Gunderman's shop, but two races into the 1997 season, a fateful call from Robbie Reiser changed everything.

Years ago, another boy racer from Arkansas toured Wisconsin. His name was Mark Martin and it seemed that he stayed 18 years old forever. Matt Kenseth has many of the same qualities. "First impression?" says Patty Butz: "Quick witted... fast thinker... bubbly... very friendly... just a bit shy."

In some ways Matt's career mirrors Jeff Gordon's. Matt's father, Roy, began to shape his career when Matt was 14 just as Gordon's stepfather began to shape Gordon's career when Jeff was very young. Like Gordon, Kenseth stays in a racing division only long enough to gain the confidence and experience needed to move on to the next level.

When he moves up, not much is expected, but he consistently delivers more than anyone might hope for.

After touring the neighbors' fields on a three-wheeler and mini-bike, after a two-year run in the sportsman division, and some 60 wins in the late model division, Matt Kenseth arrived on the Busch Grand National scene and moved up to Winston Cup. Kenseth brings to the table the smoothness, focus and talent seen in racing's champions.

Drivers gallery

**Bob
Abitz**

**Les
Back**

**Gary
Back**

**Terry
Baldry**

**Ralph
Bakewell**

**Ron
Backenberg**

**Fred
Beckler**

**Orv
Beulow**

**Fred
Bender**

**Ron
Beyer**

**Ron
Bloomberg**

**Johnny
Boegeman**

**Roy
Bohm**

**Rocky
Breezer**

**Steve
Carlson**

**Tom
Carlson**

**Ken
Christensen, Jr.**

**Arnie
Christen**

**Dave
Colby**

**Tim
Cox**

Grubba

Dan Darnell

Greg DeLapp

Morie Delmore

Jim Derhaag

Bobby Dotter

Jim Dumdey

Jerry Eckhardt

Ed Evans

Don Fowler

Doc Getzlaff

Willie Goeden

Bill Goss

La Verne Grandell

Dave Gray

Monte Gress

Bob Gunn

Ed Hoffman

Ed Holmes

Greg Holzhausen

Steve Holzhausen

Bob Iverson

Don James

Tom Jensen

Doug Johnson

Jim Johnson

Tom Jones	Bob Jusola	John Kassaus	Joe Krzykowski	Kirby Kurth
Cary Lalor	Dave Lalor	Marc Lamoreaux	Al Laufer	Tom Litchfield
Rich Lofy	Wayne Lodholz	Roger Lund	Kenny Lund	Bob Mackesey
John Meeger	Butch Miller	Steve Monn	John Mueller	Mike Murgic
Tom Musgrave	Jamie Neville	Lyle Nowak	Billy Oas	John Olson

Grubba

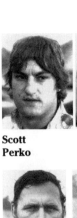
Scott
Perko

Rick
Pfrang

Jim
Piersen

Gordon
Platt

Gary
Porter

Dan
Prziborowski

George
Prziborowski

Bryan
Reffner

Royce
Rossier

Jay
Sauter

Pat
Schauer

Hub
Schulenberg

Larry
Schuler

Tracy
Schuler

Mark
Schulz

Charlie
Schwoch

Bob
Senneker

Roy
Shackelford

Rick
Smith

Boyce
Sparkman

Bruce
Sparrman

Dick
Stang

Les
Stankowski

Todd
Stapleman

Manfred
Stehli

Kevin
Stepan

Don
Stetzer

Bobby
Stolze

Bob
Strait

Doug
Strasburg

Carl
Tammi

Dave
Tomczak

Don
Turner

Bob
Turzinski

Mel
Walen

Dave
Valentyne

Rusty
Wallace

Don
Walter

Dave
Watson

Bob
Weiss

Rick
Wateski

Jim
Weber

Andy
Wendt

Bruce
White

Fred
Winn

Bob
Wisnewski

Jerry
Wood

Tim
Wood

John
Zimmerman

Marv
Zuidema

Index

Grubba